Be
Free

BE Books
by Warren Wiersbe

Be Loyal *(Matthew)*
Be Right *(Romans)*
Be Wise *(1 Corinthians)*
Be Encouraged *(2 Corinthians)*
Be Free *(Galatians)*
Be Rich *(Ephesians)*
Be Joyful *(Philippians)*
Be Complete *(Colossians)*
Be Ready *(1 & 2 Thessalonians)*
Be Faithful *(1 & 2 Timothy, Titus)*
Be Confident *(Hebrews)*
Be Mature *(James)*
Be Alert *(2 Peter, 2 & 3 John, Jude)*
Be Real *(1 John)*

Be Free

Warren W. Wiersbe

This book is designed for your personal reading pleasure and profit. It is also designed for group study. A leader's guide with helps and hints for teachers and visual aids (Victor Multiuse Transparency Masters) is available from your local bookstore or from the publisher.

 VICTOR BOOKS a division of SP Publications, Inc.
WHEATON, ILLINOIS 60187

Offices also in
Whitby, Ontario, Canada
Amersham-on-the-Hill, Bucks, England

Scripture quotations are from the Authorized (King James) Version unless indicated otherwise. Other versions quoted include *The New American Standard Bible* (NASB), © 1971, The Lockman Foundation, La Habra, Calif.; *The New International Version: New Testament* (NIV), © 1973, The New York Bible Society International; *The New Testament in the Language of the People* by Charles B. Williams (WMS), © 1966, Moody Press, Chicago, Ill. All quotations used by permission.

Library of Congress Catalog Card Number: 74-33824
ISBN: 0-89693-733-X

VICTOR BOOKS
A division of SP Publications, Inc.
Wheaton, Ill. 60187

CONTENTS

To Fred Brown, Lee Roberson,
and Lehman Strauss—
friends in the ministry
who have been
an encouragement
along the way.

PREFACE

Galatians is a dangerous book.

It exposes the most popular substitute for spiritual living that we have in our churches today—legalism. I didn't say "among the false cults." I said "in the churches" because that is where much legalism is today.

Millions of believers think they are "spiritual" because of what they don't do—or because of the leader they follow—or because of the group they belong to. The Lord shows us in Galatians how wrong we are—and how right we can be if only we would let the Holy Spirit take over.

When the Holy Spirit does take over, there will be liberty, not bondage—cooperation, not competition—glory to God, not praise to man. The world will see *true Christianity,* and sinners will come to know the Saviour. There is an old-fashioned word for this: revival.

After spending months studying Galatians, I am humbled and challenged. Humbled because I don't think God is too impressed with our ministries, no matter how impressed men may be. Challenged because I myself need to start living deeper and ministering deeper. I need to dare to let the Holy Spirit have His way, whether my life or ministry fits the current pattern or not.

So, I say: Galatians is a dangerous book. It was dangerous for Paul to write it. It was dangerous for the Galatians to read it. Perhaps my writing this

7

study of it will prove to have been a dangerous thing. (I might lose some friends and some invitations to preach!)

So be it. All I pray is that you and I will appreciate and experience the liberty we have in Christ; lest He have died in vain.

"If the Son therefore shall make you free, you shall be free indeed" (John 8:36).

My friend—BE FREE!

WARREN W. WIERSBE

Part I

Personal Section:

Grace
and the Gospel

Chapters 1—2

Galatians 1:1-10

Paul, an apostle (not of men, neither by man, but by Jesus Christ, and God the Father, who raised Him from the dead), and all the brethren which are with me, unto the churches of Galatia:

Grace be to you and peace from God the Father, and from our Lord Jesus Christ, who gave Himself for our sins, that He might deliver us from this present evil world, according to the will of God and our Father: to whom be glory for ever and ever. Amen.

I marvel that ye are so soon removed from Him that called you into the grace of Christ unto another gospel: which is not another; but there be some that trouble you, and would pervert the Gospel of Christ.

But though we, or an angel from heaven, preach any other gospel unto you than that which we have preached unto you, let him be accursed. As we said before, so say I now again, "If any man preach any other gospel unto you than that ye have received, let him be accursed."

For do I now persuade men, or God? Or do I seek to please men? For if I yet pleased men, I should not be the servant of Christ.

1

Bad News
About the Good News

The lad at my front door was trying to sell me a subscription to a weekly newspaper, and he was very persuasive. "It only costs a quarter a week," he said, "and the best thing about this newspaper is that it prints *only the good news!*"

In a world filled with trouble, it is becoming more and more difficult to find any "good news," so perhaps the newspaper was a bargain after all. To the person who has trusted Christ as Saviour, the real "good news" is the Gospel: "Christ died for our sins according to the Scriptures; . . . He was buried, and . . . He rose again the third day according to the Scriptures" (1 Cor. 15:3-4). It is the good news that sinners can be forgiven and go to heaven because of what Jesus Christ did on the cross. The Good News of salvation through faith in Christ is the most important message in the world.

This message had changed Paul's life and, through him, the lives of others. But now this message was being attacked, and Paul was out to defend the truth of the Gospel. Some false teachers had invaded the churches of Galatia—churches Paul had founded—and were teaching a different message from that which Paul had taught.

As you begin to read Paul's letter to the Galatian Christians, you can tell immediately that something is radically wrong, because he does not open his letter with his usual praise to God and prayer for the saints. He has no time! Paul is about to engage in a battle for the truth of the Gospel and the liberty of the Christian life. False teachers are spreading a false "gospel" which is a mixture of law and grace, and Paul is not going to stand by and do nothing.

How does Paul approach the Galatian Christians in his attempt to teach them the truth about the Gospel? In these opening verses, the apostle takes three definite steps as he prepares to fight this battle.

1. He Explains His Authority (1:1-5)

Later on in his letter, Paul will deal with the Galatians on the basis of affection (4:12-20); but at the outset he is careful to let them know the authority he has from the Lord. He has three sources of authority:

His ministry (1:1-2). "Paul, an apostle. . . ." In the early days of the church, God called special men to do special tasks. Among them were the *apostles*. The word means "one who is sent with a commission." While He was ministering on earth, Jesus had many *disciples* ("learners"), and from these He selected 12 *apostles* (Mark 3:13-19). Later, one of the requirements for an apostle was that he have witnessed the resurrection (Acts 1:21-22; 2:32; 3:15). Of course, Paul himself was neither a disciple nor an apostle during Christ's earthly ministry, but he had seen the risen Lord and been commissioned by Him (Acts 9:1-18; 1 Cor. 9:1).

Paul's miraculous conversion and call to apostleship created some problems. From the very beginning, he was apart from the original apostles. His enemies said that he was not a true apostle for this reason. Paul is careful to point out that he had been made an apostle by Jesus Christ just as much as had the original Twelve. His apostleship was not from human selection and approval, but by divine appointment. Therefore, he had the authority to deal with the problems in the Galatian churches.

But in his ministry, Paul had a second basis for authority: *he had founded the churches in Galatia.* He was not writing to them as a stranger, but as the one who had brought them the message of life in the beginning! This letter reveals Paul's affection for these believers (see 4:12-19). Unfortunately, this affection was not being returned to him.

This matter of the founding of the Galatian churches has kept serious Bible students at work for many years. The problem stems from the meaning of the word *Galatia.* Several hundred years before the birth of Christ, some fierce tribes migrated from Gaul (modern France) into Asia Minor, and founded Galatia, which simply means "the country of the Gauls." When the Romans reorganized the ancient world, they made Galatia a part of a larger province that included several other areas, and they called the entire province Galatia. So, back in Paul's day, when a person talked about Galatia, you could not be sure whether he meant the smaller country of Galatia or the larger Roman province.

Bible students are divided over whether Paul wrote to churches in the *country* of Galatia or in the *province* of Galatia. The former view is called the "north Galatian theory" and the latter the "south Galatian theory." The matter is not finally settled, but the evidence seems to indicate that Paul wrote to churches in the southern part of the province of Galatia—Antioch, Iconium, Lystra, Derbe—churches he founded on his first missionary journey (Acts 13—14).

Paul always had a loving concern for his converts and a deep desire to see the churches he had founded glorify Christ (see Acts 15:36; 2 Cor. 11:28). He was not content to lead men and women to Christ and then abandon them. (For an example of his "after-care," read 1 Thes. 2.)

When Paul heard that false teachers had begun to capture his converts and lead them astray, he was greatly concerned—and rightly so. After all, teaching new Christians how to live for Christ is as much a part of Christ's commission as winning them (Matt. 28:19-20). Sad to say, many of the Galatian Christians had turned away from Paul, their "spiritual father" in the Lord, and were now following legalistic teachers who were mixing Old Testament Law with the Gospel of God's grace. (We call these false teachers "Judaizers" because they were trying to entice Christians back into the Jewish religious system.)

So, Paul had a ministry as an apostle, and specifically as the founder of the Galatian churches. As such, he had the authority to deal with the problems in the churches. But there was a second source of authority:

His message (1:3-4). From the very beginning, Paul clearly states the message of the Gospel, because it was this message that the Judaizers were changing. The Gospel centers in *a Person*—Jesus Christ, the Son of God. This Person paid *a price*

—He gave Himself to die on the cross. (You will discover that the cross is important in the Galatian letter, see 2:19-21; 3:1, 13; 4:5; 5:11, 24; 6:12-14.) Christ paid the price that He might achieve *a purpose*—delivering sinners from bondage.

"Liberty in Christ" is the dominant theme of Galatians. (Check the word *bondage* in 2:4; 4:3, 9, 24-25; 5:1.) The Judaizers wanted to lead the Christians out of the liberty of grace into the bondage of law. Paul knew that bondage was not a part of the message of the Gospel, for Christ had died to set men free.

Paul's ministry and message were sources of spiritual authority, but so also was:

His motive (1:5). "To whom be glory for ever and ever!" The false teachers were not ministering for the glory of Christ, but for their own glory (see 6:12-14). Like false teachers today, the Judaizers were not busy winning lost people to Christ. Rather, they were stealing other men's converts and bragging about their statistics. But Paul's motive was pure and godly: he wanted to glorify Jesus Christ (see 1 Cor. 6:19-20; 10:31-33).

Paul has now explained his authority. He is ready for a second step as he begins this battle for the liberty of the Christian.

2. He Expresses His Anxiety (1:6-7)

"I am amazed that you are so quickly moving away!" This is the first reason for Paul's anxiety: the Galatians were *deserting the grace of God.* (The verb indicates they were in the process of deserting and had not fully turned away.)

Paul strikes while the iron is hot. God had called them in His grace, and saved them from their sins. Now they are moving from grace back into law. They are abandoning liberty for legalism! And they are doing it so quickly, without consulting Paul, their "spiritual father," or giving time for the Holy Spirit to teach them. They have become infatuated with the religion of the Judaizers, just the way little children follow a stranger because he offers them candy.

"The grace of God" is a basic theme in this letter (1:3, 6, 15; 2:9, 21; 5:4; 6:18). Grace is simply God's favor to undeserving sinners. The words "grace" and "gift" go together, because salvation is the gift of God through His grace (Eph. 2:8-10). The Galatian believers were not simply "changing religions" or "changing churches" but were actually abandoning the very grace of God! To make matters worse, they were deserting the very God of grace! God had called them and saved them; now they were deserting Him for human leaders who would bring them into bondage.

We must never forget that the Christian life is a living relationship with God through Jesus Christ. A man does not become a Christian merely by agreeing to a set of doctrines; he becomes a Christian by submitting to Christ and trusting Him (Rom. 11:6). You cannot mix grace and works, because the one excludes the other. Salvation is the gift of God's grace, purchased for us by Jesus Christ on the cross. To turn from grace to law is to desert the God who saved us.

But they were guilty of another sin that gave Paul great anxiety: *they were perverting the Gospel of God*. The Judaizers claimed to be preaching "the Gospel," but there cannot be two gospels, one centered in works and the other centered in grace. "They are not preaching another gospel," writes Paul, "but a *different* message—one so different

from the true Gospel that it is no gospel at all."
Like the cultists today, the Judaizers would say,
"We believe in Jesus Christ—*but* we have something wonderful *to add* to what you already believe." As if any man could "add" something better
to the grace of God!

The word translated *pervert* in verse 7 is used
only three times in the New Testament (Acts 2:20;
James 4:9; Gal. 1:7). It means "to turn about, to
change into an opposite character." The word could
be translated "to reverse." In other words, the
Judaizers had reversed the Gospel—they had
turned it around and taken it back into the Law!
Later in this letter, Paul explains how the law was
preparation for the coming of Christ, but the Judaizers had a different interpretation. To them, the
law and the Gospel went together. "Except ye be
circumcised after the manner [law] of Moses, ye
cannot be saved" (Acts 15:1).

What was this "deserting and perverting" doing
to the Galatian Christians? It was troubling them
(Gal. 1:7). This verb *trouble* carries with it the
idea of perplexity, confusion, and unrest. You get
some idea of the force of this word when you see
how it is used in other places. *Trouble* describes
the feelings of the disciples in the ship during the
storm (Matt. 14:26). It also describes the feelings
of King Herod when he heard that a new king had
been born (Matt. 2:3). No wonder Paul was anxious for his converts: they were going through
great agitation because of the false doctrines that
had been brought to the churches. Grace always
leads to peace (see Gal. 1:3), but the believers
had deserted grace and therefore had no peace in
their hearts.

Keep in mind that God's grace involves something more than man's salvation. We not only are saved by grace, but we are to live by grace (1 Cor. 15:10). We stand in grace; it is the foundation for the Christian life (Rom. 5:1-2). Grace gives us the strength we need to be victorious soldiers (2 Tim. 2:1-4). Grace enables us to suffer without complaining, and even to use that suffering for God's glory (2 Cor. 12:1-10). When a Christian turns away from living by God's grace, he must depend on his own power. This leads to failure and disappointment. This is what Paul means by "fallen from grace" (Gal. 5:4)—moving out of the sphere of grace into the sphere of law, ceasing to depend on God's resources and depending on our own resources.

No wonder Paul was anxious. His friends in Christ were deserting the God of grace, perverting the grace of God, and reverting to living by the flesh and their own resources. They had begun their Christian lives in the Spirit, but now they were going to try to continue them in the power of the flesh (Gal. 3:3).

Having explained his authority and expressed his anxiety, Paul now takes the third step:

3. He Exposes His Adversaries (1:8-10)

"Make love, not war!" may have been a popular slogan, but it is not always feasible. Doctors must make war against disease and death; sanitary engineers must war against filth and pollution; legislators must war against injustice and crime. And they all fight *because of something they love!*

"Ye that love the Lord, hate evil" (Ps. 97:10). "Abhor that which is evil; cleave to that which is good" (Rom. 12:9). Paul waged war against the false teachers because he loved the truth, and be-

cause he loved those whom he had led to Christ.
Like a loving father who guards his daughter until she is married, Paul watched over his converts
lest they be seduced into sin (2 Cor. 11:1-4).

The Judaizers are identified by *the false gospel
that they preached*. The test of a man's ministry
is not popularity (Matt. 24:11), or miraculous
signs and wonders (Matt. 24:23-24), but his faithfulness to the Word of God (see Isa. 8:20; 1 Tim. 4;
1 John 4:1-6; and note that 2 John 5-11 warns us
not to encourage those who bring false doctrine).
Christ had committed the Gospel to Paul (1 Cor.
15:1-8), and he, in turn, had committed it to other
faithful servants (1 Tim. 1:11 and 6:20; 2 Tim. 1:13
and 2:2). But the Judaizers had come along and
substituted their false gospel for the true Gospel,
and for this sin, Paul pronounced them accursed.
The word he uses is *anathema,* which means "dedi-
cated to destruction." (Read Acts 23:14 for a force-
ful illustration of the meaning of this word.) No
matter who the preacher may be—an angel from
heaven or even Paul himself—if he preaches any
other gospel, he is accursed!

But there is a second characteristic of Paul's adversaries: *the false motives that they practiced*.
His enemies accused Paul of being a compromiser
and "adjusting" the Gospel to fit the Gentiles.
Perhaps they twisted the meaning of Paul's statement, "I am made all things to all men, that I might
by all means save some" (1 Cor. 9:22). They said,
"When Paul is with the Jews, he lives like a Jew;
but when he is with the Gentiles, he lives like the
Gentiles. He is a man-pleaser, and therefore you
cannot trust him!"

But in reality, it was the false teacher who was
the man-pleaser. "These men are paying you spe-

cial attention, but not sincerely," Paul wrote
(4:17). "They want to shut you off from me, so
that you may keep on paying them special attention" (WMS). Later, Paul also exposes the false
teachers as the compromisers, going back to Old
Testament practices so that they would not be
persecuted by the Jewish people (6:12-15). Paul
was definitely *not* a man-pleaser. His *ministry* did
not come from man (1:1), nor did his *message*
come from man (1:12). Why, then, should he be
afraid of men? Why should he seek to please men?
His heart's desire was to please Christ.

When Verdi produced his first opera in Florence,
the composer stood by himself in the shadows and
kept his eye on the face of one man in the audience
—the great Rossini. It mattered not to Verdi
whether the people in the hall were cheering him
or jeering him; all he wanted was a smile of approval from the master musician. So it was with
Paul. He knew what it was to suffer for the Gospel,
but the approval or disapproval of men did not
move him. "Therefore also we have as our ambition . . . to be pleasing to Him" (2 Cor. 5:9, NASB).
Paul wanted the approval of Christ.

The servant of God is constantly tempted to
compromise in order to attract and please men.
When D. L. Moody was preaching in England, a
worker came to him on the platform and told him
that a very important nobleman had come into the
hall. "May the meeting be a blessing to him!" was
Moody's reply, and he preached just as before,
without trying to impress anybody.

Paul was not a politician; he was an ambassador.
His task was not to "play politics" but to proclaim a
message. These Judaizers, on the other hand, were
cowardly compromisers who mixed law and grace,

hoping to please both Jews and Gentiles, but never asking whether or not they were pleasing God.

We have noted three steps Paul took toward engaging these false teachers in battle: he explained his authority, expressed his anxiety, and exposed his adversaries. But how is he going to attack his enemies? What approach will he use to convince the Galatian believers that all they need is faith in God's grace? A quick survey of the entire letter shows that Paul is a master defender of the Gospel. Take time to read the entire letter at one sitting, and, as you read, note the three approaches that Paul takes.

His first approach is *personal* (chaps. 1-2). He reviews his own personal experience with Jesus Christ and the message of the Gospel. He points out that he had received the Gospel independently, from the Lord and not from the 12 apostles (1:11-24), but that they had approved his message and his ministry (2:1-10). Furthermore, Paul had even defended the Gospel when Peter, the leading apostle, had compromised his earlier stand (2:11-21). The autobiographical section of the letter proves that Paul was not a "counterfeit apostle," but that his message and ministry were true to the faith.

Chapters 3 and 4 are *doctrinal,* and in them Paul presents several arguments to establish that sinners are saved by faith and grace, not by works and law. First he appeals to their own experiences (3:1-5). Then he goes back to the Old Testament law in 3:6-14 to show that even Abraham and the prophets understood salvation as being by grace through faith. Having mentioned the law, Paul now explains why the law was given originally (3:15—4:18). He then uses the story of Sarah and Hagar to illustrate the relationship of law and grace (4:19-31).

The final two chapters of the letter are *practical* in emphasis, as Paul turns from argument to application. The Judaizers accused Paul of promoting lawlessness because he preached the Gospel of the grace of God; so in this section, Paul explains the relationship between the grace of God and practical Christian living. He shows that living by grace means liberty, not bondage (5:1-12); depending on the Spirit, not the flesh (5:13-26); living for others, not for self (6:1-10); and living for the glory of God, not for man's approval (6:11-18). It is either one series of actions or the other—law or grace—but it cannot be both.

The Galatian letter is not a book to be taken lightly. Galatians was Martin Luther's charter of liberty during the Reformation. Luther's writings, in turn, brought the truth of salvation by faith to John Wesley's heart in that little meeting on Aldersgate Street in London on May 24, 1738. It was Wesley whom God used in such a remarkable way to spearhead revival in the British Isles, leading eventually to the founding of the Methodist Church. And that revival positively affected the entire English-speaking world. As we study Galatians, we are participating in a tremendous spiritual chain reaction that even today could result in another revival.

A Suggested Outline of Galatians

Theme: Christian liberty in the grace of God (5:1)

I. PERSONAL: GRACE AND THE
   GOSPEL—chapters 1—2
   1. Grace declared in Paul's message—1:1-10
   2. Grace demonstrated in Paul's life—1:11-24
   3. Grace defended in Paul's ministry—2:1-21
      (1) Before the church collectively—2:1-10
      (2) Before Peter personally—2:11-21

II. DOCTRINAL: GRACE AND THE LAW—
    chapters 3—4
    1. The personal argument—3:1-5
    2. The scriptural argument—3:6-14
    3. The logical argument—3:15-29
    4. The historical argument—4:1-11
    5. The sentimental argument—4:12-18
    6. The allegorical argument—4:19-31

III. PRACTICAL: GRACE AND THE
     CHRISTIAN LIFE—chapters 5—6
     1. Liberty, not bondage—5:1-12
     2. The Spirit, not the flesh—5:13-26
     3. Others, not self—6:1-10
     4. God's glory, not man's praise—6:11-18

Galatians 1:11-24

But I certify you, brethren, that the Gospel which was preached of me is not after man. For I neither received it of man, neither was I taught it, but by revelation of Jesus Christ.

For ye have heard of my conversation in time past in the Jews' religion, how that beyond measure I persecuted the church of God, and wasted it:

And profited in the Jews' religion above many my equals in mine own nation, being more exceedingly zealous of the traditions of my fathers.

But when it pleased God, who separated me from my mother's womb, and called me by His grace, to reveal His Son in me, that I might preach Him among the heathen;

Immediately I conferred not with flesh and blood: Neither went I up to Jerusalem to them which were apostles before me; but I went into Arabia, and returned again unto Damascus.

Then after three years I went up to Jerusalem to see Peter, and abode with him 15 days. But other of the apostles saw I none, save James the Lord's brother.

Now the things which I write unto you, behold, before God, I lie not.

Afterwards I came into the regions of Syria and Cilicia; and was unknown by face unto the churches of Judea which were in Christ: but they had heard only, that he which persecuted us in times past now preacheth the faith which once he destroyed.

And they glorified God in me.

2

Born Free!

"Whoso would be a man must be a nonconformist." So wrote Emerson, and many a thinker agrees with him.

The English art critic John Ruskin said, "I fear uniformity. You cannot manufacture great men any more than you can manufacture gold."

The German philosopher Schopenhauer wrote, "We forfeit three-fourths of ourselves in order to be like other people."

Francis Asbury, first bishop of the Methodist Church in the United States, once prayed at a deacon ordination, "O Lord, grant that these brethren may never want to be like other people."

Of course, there is a wrong kind of individualism that destroys instead of fulfills; but in a society accustomed to interchanging parts, it is good to meet a man like Paul who dared to be himself in the will of God. But his freedom in Christ was a threat to those who found safety in conformity.

Paul's enemies pointed to his nonconformity as proof that his message and ministry were not really of God. "He claims to be an apostle," they argued,

"but he does not stand in the apostolic tradition."
It is this misrepresentation that Paul answers in
this section of Galatians. His nonconformity was
divinely deliberate. God had chosen to reveal Himself in a different way to Paul.

In verses 11 and 12, Paul states his theme: his
message and ministry are of divine origin. He did
not invent the Gospel, nor did he receive it from
men; but he received the Gospel from Jesus Christ.
Both his message and his apostolic ministry were
divinely given. Therefore, anybody who added
anything to Paul's Gospel was in danger of divine
judgment, because that Gospel was given by Jesus
Christ from heaven (1 Cor. 15:1-11).

The best way for Paul to prove his point is to
reach into his past and remind the Galatian Christians of the way God had dealt with him. Paul
states that his past life was already known to his
readers (Gal. 1:13), but it was obvious that they
did not fully understand what those experiences
meant. So, Paul flashes on the screen three pictures
from his past as evidence that his apostleship and
his Gospel are truly of God.

1. The Persecutor (1:13-14)

Paul begins with his past conduct as an unconverted Jewish rabbi. (For a vivid account of these
years from Paul's own lips, read Acts 22 and 26,
as well as Acts 9.) In this historical flashback, Paul
points out his relationship to the church (v. 13)
and to the religion of the Jews (v. 14). He was
persecuting the church and profiting and progress-
ing in the Jewish religion. Everything was "going
his way" and he was rapidly being recognized as
a spiritual leader in Israel.

It is interesting to note the words that are used

to describe Paul's activities when he was "Saul of Tarsus" persecuting the church. He "consented" to the murder of Stephen (see Acts 8:1), and then proceeded to "make havoc of the church" (see Acts 8:3) by breaking up families and putting believers in prison. The very atmosphere that he breathed was "threatening and slaughter" (Acts 9:1). So bent on destroying the church was Paul that he voted to kill the believers (Acts 22:4-5; 26:9-11). He mentions these facts in his letters (1 Cor. 15:9; Phil. 3:6; 1 Tim. 1:13), marveling that God could save such a sinner as he.

Paul actually thought that Jesus was an impostor and His message of salvation a lie. He was sure that God had spoken through Moses, but how could he be sure that God had spoken through Jesus of Nazareth? Steeped in Jewish tradition, young Saul of Tarsus championed his faith. His reputation as a zealous persecutor of "the sect of the Nazarenes" became known far and wide (see Acts 9:13-14). Everybody knew that this brilliant student of Rabbi Gamaliel (Acts 22:3) was well on his way to becoming an influential leader of the Jewish faith. His personal religious life, his scholarship (Acts 26:24), and his zeal in opposing alien religious faiths, all combined to make him the most respected young rabbi of his day.

Then something happened: Saul of Tarsus, the persecutor of the church, became Paul the Apostle, the preacher of the Gospel. This change was not gradual; it happened suddenly and without warning (Acts 9:1-9). Saul was on his way to Damascus to persecute the Christians; a few days later he was in Damascus preaching to the Jews that the Christians are right. How could the Judaizers explain this sudden transformation?

Was Saul's remarkable "about face" caused by his own people, the Jews? Unthinkable! The Jews were encouraging Saul in his program of persecution, and his conversion was an embarrassment to them.

Was Saul's change caused by the Christians he was persecuting? Certainly the believers prayed for him, and no doubt the death of Stephen—and especially the glorious testimony he had given—affected Paul deeply (Acts 22:19-20). But the Christians ran from Paul (Acts 8:1, 4; 9:10-16), and, as far as we know, they had no idea that the young rabbi would ever become a Christian.

But if the amazing change in Paul was not caused by the Jews or the church, *then who caused it?* It had to come from God!

No matter how you look at it, the conversion of Paul was a spiritual miracle. It was humanly impossible for Rabbi Saul to become the Apostle Paul apart from the miracle of God's grace. And the same God who saved Paul also called him to be an apostle, and gave him the message of the Gospel. *For the Judaizers to deny Paul's apostleship and Gospel was the same as denying his conversion!* Certainly Paul was preaching the same message that he himself had believed—the truth that had changed him. But no mere human message could effect such a change. Paul's argument is conclusive: his past conduct as a persecutor of the church plus the dramatic change that he experienced prove that his message and ministry are from God.

2. The Believer (1:15-16b, 24)

Having discussed his past character and conduct, Paul now explains his conversion; for, after all, this was the crucial thing in his life. "What I preach to others, I have experienced myself," he is saying to his accusers. "This is the true Gospel. Any other Gospel is counterfeit." In these verses Paul explains the characteristics of his conversion experience.

God did it (1:15a, 16a). "It pleased God . . . to reveal His Son in me." Whenever Paul spoke or wrote about his conversion, it was always with emphasis on the fact that God did the work. "Salvation is of the Lord!" (Jonah 2:9)

God did it by grace (1:15b). Paul's experience reminds us of young Jeremiah (Jer. 1:4-10) and also of John the Baptist (Luke 1:5-17). Salvation is by God's grace, not man's efforts or character. *Grace* and *called* (Gal. 1:15b) go together, for whomever God chooses in His grace He calls through His Word (1 Thes. 1:4-5). The mysteries of God's sovereign will and man's responsibility to obey are not fully revealed to us. We do know that God is "not willing that any should perish" (2 Peter 3:9), and that those who do trust Christ discover they have been "chosen . . . in Him before the foundation of the world" (Eph. 1:4).

God did it through Christ (1:16a). In another letter Paul makes it clear that he had plenty to boast about when he was an unconverted man (Phil. 3). He had religion and self-righteousness, as well as reputation and recognition; *but he did not have Christ!* When on the Damascus Road, Paul saw his own self-righteous rags contrasted to the righteousness of Christ, he realized what he was missing. "But what things were gain to me, those I counted loss for Christ" (Phil. 3:7).

God revealed Christ *to* Paul, *in* Paul, and *through* Paul. The "Jews' religion" (Gal. 1:14) had been an experience of outward rituals and practices; but faith in Christ brought about an inward experience of reality with the Lord. This "inward-ness" of Christ is a major truth with Paul (Gal. 2:20; 4:19).

God did it for the sake of others (1:16b). God chose Paul, not only to save him, but also to use him to win others. In the Bible, the doctrine of election is never taught with a view to producing pride or selfishness. Election involves responsibility. God chose Paul to preach among the Gentiles the same grace that he had experienced. This, in it-self, was evidence that Paul's conversion was of God; for certainly a prejudiced Jewish rabbi would never decide of himself to minister to the despised Gentiles! (See Acts 9:15; 15:12; 22:21-22; Eph. 3:1, 8.)

God did it for His glory (1:24). As a fanatical rabbi, Paul had all the glory a man could want; but what he was doing did not glorify God. Man was *created* to glorify God (Isa. 43:7) and man is *saved* to glorify God (1 Cor. 6:19-20). Bringing glory to God was ever a compelling motive in Paul's life and ministry (Rom. 11:36; 16:27; Eph. 1:6; 3:20-21; Phil. 4:20; 1 Cor. 10:31). The Judaizers were interested in their own glory (Gal. 6:11-18). That is why they were stealing Paul's converts and leading them astray. If Paul had been interested in glorifying himself, he could have remained a Jew-ish rabbi and perhaps become Gamaliel's successor. But it was the glory of God that motivated Paul, and this ought to motivate our lives as well.

When Charles Haddon Spurgeon was a young preacher, his father, the Rev. John Spurgeon, sug-gested that Charles go to college to gain promi-nence. It was arranged for him to meet Dr. Joseph Angus, the principal of Stepney College, London. They were to meet at Mr. Macmillan's home in

Cambridge, and Spurgeon was there at the appointed hour. He waited for two hours, but the learned doctor never appeared. When Spurgeon finally inquired about the man, he discovered that Dr. Angus had been waiting in another room and, because of another appointment, had already departed. Disappointed, Spurgeon left for a preaching engagement. While he was walking along, he heard a voice clearly say to him, "Seekest thou great things for thyself? Seek them not!" (See Jer. 45:5.) From that moment, Spurgeon determined to do the will of God for the glory of God; and God blessed him in an exceptional way.

Paul has pictured himself as a persecutor, and has reviewed his character and conduct. He has also pictured himself as a believer, reviewing his conversion. He now presents a third picture.

3. The Preacher (1:16c-23)

What were Paul's contacts with other believers after he was converted? This is a question vital to his defense. Paul had no personal contacts with the apostles right after his conversion experience on the Damascus Road. "Immediately I conferred not with flesh and blood" (Gal. 1:16c). The logical thing for Paul to have done after his conversion was to introduce himself to the church at Jerusalem and profit from the spiritual instruction of those who had been "in Christ" before him. But this he did not do—and his decision was led of the Lord. For if he had gone to Jerusalem, his ministry might have been identified with that of the apostles—all Jews—and this could have been a hindrance to his work among the Gentiles.

At this point we need to remind ourselves that the message of the Gospel came "to the Jew first"

(Acts 3:26; Rom. 1:16). Our Lord's ministry was to the nation of Israel, and so was the ministry of the apostles for the first few years (see Acts 1—7). The death of Stephen was a turning point. As the believers were scattered, they took the Good News with them to other places (Acts 8:4; 11:19 ff.). Philip took the message to the Samaritans (Acts 8), and then God directed Peter to introduce it to the Gentiles (Acts 10). However, it remained for Paul to carry the Gospel to the Gentile masses (Acts 22:21-22; Eph. 3:1, 8), and for this reason God kept him separated from the predominantly Jewish ministry being conducted by the apostles in Jerusalem.

Paul did not immediately go to Jerusalem. Where did he go? He reviews his contacts and shows that there was no opportunity for him to receive either his message or his apostolic calling from any of the leaders of the church. (Compare this section with Acts 9:10-31, and keep in mind that even the best biblical scholars are not agreed on the chronology of Paul's life. Fortunately, the details of history do not affect the understanding of what Paul has written: we can disagree on chronology and yet agree on theology!)

He went to Arabia (1:17b). This was after his initial ministry in Damascus (Acts 9:19-20). Instead of "conferring with flesh and blood," Paul gave himself to study, prayer, and meditation, and met with the Lord alone. He may have spent the greater part of three years in Arabia (Gal. 1:18), and no doubt was involved in evangelism as well as personal spiritual growth. The apostles had received three years of teaching from the Lord Jesus, and now Paul was going to have his own opportunity to be taught of the Lord.

He went back to Damascus (1:17c). It would have been logical to visit Jerusalem at this point, but the Lord directed otherwise. Certainly it was a risky thing for Paul to go back to the city that knew he had become a Christian. The Jewish leaders who had looked to him as their champion against Christianity would definitely be after his blood. Apparently the "basket incident" of Acts 9:23-25 (see 2 Cor. 11:32-33) took place at this time. The return to Damascus and the danger it brought to Paul's life are further proof that the Jewish leaders considered Paul an enemy, and therefore that his experience with Christ was a valid one.

He finally visited Jerusalem (1:18-20). This was three years after his conversion, and his main purpose was to visit Peter. But Paul had a tough time getting into the church fellowship! (Acts 9:26-28) If his message and ministry had been from the apostles, this would never have happened; but because Paul's experience had been with the Lord Jesus alone, the apostles were suspicious of him. He stayed in Jerusalem only 15 days, and he saw only Peter and James (the Lord's brother). Thus he received neither his message nor his apostleship from the Jerusalem church. There simply was not the time nor the opportunity. He had already received them both directly from Christ.

He returned home to Tarsus (1:21-23). Again, the record in Acts explains why: his life was in danger in Jerusalem, just as it had been in Damascus (Acts 9:28-30). As Paul went through Syria, he preached the Word, and when he arrived in Cilicia, his home province (Acts 21:39; 22:3), he began to evangelize (see Acts 15:23). Historians have concluded that he remained there perhaps seven years, until Barnabas recruited him for the work in Antioch (Acts 11:19-26). A few believers in Jerusalem knew Paul, but the believers in the churches of Judea did not know him, though they heard that he was now preaching the very faith he had once tried to destroy.

In the light of Paul's conduct, his conversion, and his contacts, how could anybody accuse him of borrowing or inventing either his message or his ministry? Certainly he *did* receive his Gospel by a revelation from Jesus Christ. Therefore, we must be careful what we do with this Gospel, for it is not the invention of men, but the very truth of God.

Some critical scholars have accused Paul of "corrupting the simple Gospel," but the evidence is against this accusation. *The same Christ who taught on earth also taught through Paul from heaven.* Paul did not invent his teaching; he "received" it (Rom. 1:5; 1 Cor. 11:23; 15:3). At the time of Paul's conversion, God said He would appear to him in the future (Acts 26:16), apparently for the purpose of revealing His truths to him. This means that the Christ of the four Gospels and the Christ of the epistles is the same Person; there is no conflict between Christ and Paul. When Paul wrote his letters to the churches, he put his own teaching on the same level with that of Jesus Christ (2 Thes. 3:3-15). The Apostle Peter even calls Paul's letters "Scripture" (2 Peter 3:15-16).

Modern-day "Judaizers," like their ancient counterparts, reject the authority of Paul and try to undermine the Gospel which he preached. In Paul's day, their message was "the Gospel *plus* Moses." In our day it is "the Gospel *plus*" any number of religious leaders, religious books, or religious organizations. "You cannot be saved unless . . ." is their message (Acts 15:1); and that "unless" usually includes joining their group and obeying their rules. If you dare to mention the Gospel of grace as preached by Jesus, Paul, and the other apostles, they reply, "But God has given us a new revelation!"

Paul has the answer for them: "If any man preach any other gospel unto you than that ye have received, let him be accursed!" (Gal. 1:9) When a sinner trusts Christ and is born again (John 3:1-18), he is "born free." He has been redeemed—purchased by Christ and set free. He is no longer in bondage to sin or Satan, nor should he be in bondage to human religious systems (Gal. 4:1-11; 5:1). "If the Son therefore shall make you free, ye shall be free indeed" (John 8:36).

Galatians 2:1-10

Then 14 years after, I went up again to Jerusalem with Barnabas, and took Titus with me also. And I went up by revelation, and communicated unto them that Gospel which I preach among the Gentiles, but privately to them which were of reputation, lest by any means I should run, or had run, in vain.

But neither Titus, who was with me, being a Greek, was compelled to be circumcised: And that because of false brethren unawares brought in, who came in privily to spy out our liberty which we have in Christ Jesus, that they might bring us into bondage: To whom we gave place by subjection, no, not for an hour; that the truth of the Gospel might continue with you.

But of these who seemed to be somewhat (whatsoever they were, it maketh no matter to me: God accepteth no man's person), for they who seemed to be somewhat in conference added nothing to me. But contrariwise, when they saw that the Gospel of the uncircumcision was committed unto me, as the Gospel of the circumcision was unto Peter (for He that wrought effectually in Peter to the apostleship of the circumcision, the same was mighty in me toward the Gentiles). And when James, Cephas, and John, who seemed to be pillars, perceived the grace that was given unto me, they gave to me and Barnabas the right hands of fellowship; that we should go unto the heathen, and they unto the circumcision.

Only they would that we should remember the poor; the same which I also was forward to do.

3

The Freedom Fighter, Part I

"This will remain the land of the free only so long as it is the home of the brave."

So wrote veteran news analyst Elmer Davis in his book *But We Were Born Free,* and his convictions would certainly be echoed by the Apostle Paul. To Paul, his spiritual liberty in Christ was worth far more than popularity or even security. He was willing to fight for that liberty.

Paul's first fight for Christian liberty was at the Jerusalem Council (Gal. 2:1-10; Acts 15:1-35); his second was at a private meeting with Peter (Gal. 2:11-21). Had Paul been unwilling to wage this spiritual warfare, the church in the first century might have become only a Jewish sect, preaching a mixture of law and grace. But because of Paul's courage, the Gospel was kept free from legalism, and it was carried to the Gentiles with great blessing.

Before we look at the three acts in the first drama, the council at Jerusalem, we must get acquainted with the participants. *Paul,* of course, we know as the great apostle to the Gentiles.

Barnabas was one of Paul's closest friends. In fact, when Paul tried to get into the fellowship of the Jerusalem church, it was Barnabas who opened the way for him (Acts 9:26-28).

The name *Barnabas* means "son of encouragement," and you will always find Barnabas encouraging somebody. When the Gospel came to the Gentiles in Antioch, it was Barnabas who was sent to encourage them in their faith (Acts 11:19-24).

Thus, from the earliest days, Barnabas was associated with the Gentile believers. It was Barnabas who enlisted Paul to help minister at the church in Antioch (Acts 11:25-26), and the two of them worked together, not only in teaching, but also in helping the poor (Acts 11:27-30).

Barnabas accompanied Paul on the first missionary trip (Acts 13:1—14:28) and had seen God's blessings on the Gospel that they preached. It is worth noting that it was Barnabas who encouraged young John Mark after he had "dropped out" of the ministry and incurred the displeasure of Paul (Acts 13:13; 15:36-41). In later years, Paul was able to commend Mark and benefit from his friendship (Col. 4:10; 2 Tim. 4:11).

Titus was a Gentile believer who worked with Paul and apparently was won to Christ through the apostle's ministry (Titus 1:4). He was a "product" of the apostle's ministry among the Gentiles, and was taken to the Jerusalem conference as "exhibit A" from the Gentile churches. In later years, Titus assisted Paul by going to some of the most difficult churches to help them solve their problems (2 Cor. 7; Titus 1:5).

Three men were the "pillars" of the church in Jerusalem: Peter, John, and James, the brother of the Lord (who must not be confused with the

Apostle James, who was killed by Herod, Acts 12:1-2). *Peter* we know from his prominent part in the accounts in the Gospels as well as in the first half of the Book of Acts. It was to Peter that Jesus gave "the keys," so that it was he who was involved in opening the door of faith to the Jews (Acts 2), the Samaritans (Acts 8), and the Gentiles (Acts 10). *John* we also know from the Gospel records as one of Christ's "inner three" apostles, associated with Peter in the ministry of the Word (Acts 3:1 ff.).

It is *James* who perhaps needs more introduction. The Gospel record indicates that Mary and Joseph had other children, and James was among them (Matt. 13:55; Mark 6:3). (Of course, Jesus was born by the power of the Spirit, and not through natural generation; Matt. 1:18-25; Luke 1:26-38.) Our Lord's brothers and sisters did not believe in Him during His earthly ministry (John 7:1-5). Yet we find "His brethren" associated with the believers in the Early Church (Acts 1:13-14). Paul informs us that the risen Christ appeared to James, and this was the turning point in his life (1 Cor. 15:5-7). James was the leader of the Early Church in Jerusalem (Acts 15; see also 21:18). He was also the writer of the Epistle of James; and that letter, plus Acts 21:18, would suggest that he was very Jewish in his thinking.

Along with these men, and the "apostles and elders" (Acts 15:4, 6), were a group of "false brethren" who infiltrated the meetings and tried to rob the believers of their liberty in Christ (Gal. 2:4). Undoubtedly these were some of the Judaizers who had followed Paul in church after church and had tried to capture his converts. The fact that Paul calls them "false brethren" indicates that they were not true Christians, but were only masquerading as such so they could capture the conference for themselves.

This, then, is the cast of characters. Acts 15 should be read along with Galatians 2:1-10 to get the full story of the event.

Act 1—The Private Consultation (2:1-2)

Paul and Barnabas had returned to Antioch from their first missionary journey, excited about the way God had "opened the door of faith unto the Gentiles" (Acts 14:27). But the Jewish legalists in Jerusalem were upset with their report; so they came to Antioch and taught, in effect, that a Gentile had to become a Jew before he could become a Christian (Acts 15:1).

Circumcision, which they demanded of the Gentiles, was an important Jewish rite, handed down from the days of Abraham (Gen. 17). Submitting to circumcision meant accepting and obeying the whole Jewish law. Actually, the Jewish people had forgotten the inner, spiritual meaning of the rite (Deut. 10:16; Jer. 4:1-4; Rom. 2:25-29), just as some churches today have lost the spiritual meaning of baptism and have turned it into an external ritual. The true Christian has experienced an inner circumcision of the heart (Col. 2:10-11) and does not need to submit to any physical operation (Phil. 3:1-3).

When Paul and Barnabas confronted these men with the truth of the Gospel, the result was a heated argument (Acts 15:2). It was decided that the best place to settle the question was before the church leaders in Jerusalem. We should not think that this "Jerusalem Conference" was a representative meeting from all the churches, such as a denominational conference; it was not. Paul,

Barnabas, Titus, and certain other men from Antioch represented the Gentile Christians who had
been saved totally apart from Jewish law; but there
were no representatives from the churches Paul
had established in Gentile territory.

When the deputation arrived in Jerusalem, they
met privately with the church leaders. Paul did not
go to Jerusalem because the church sent him; he
"went up by revelation"—that is, the Lord sent him
(compare Gal. 2:1 and 1:12). And the Lord gave
him the wisdom to meet with the leaders first so
that they would be able to present a united front
at the public meetings.

"Lest by any means I should run, or had run, in
vain" (v. 2) does not mean that Paul was unsure
either of his message or his ministry. His conduct
on the way to the conference indicates that he had
no doubts (Acts 15:3). What he was concerned
about was the future of the Gospel among the Gentiles, because this was his specific ministry from
Christ. If the "pillars" sided with the Judaizers, or
tried to compromise, then Paul's ministry would be
in jeopardy. He wanted to get their approval *before* he faced the whole assembly; otherwise a
three-way division could result.

What was the result of this private consultation?
The apostles and elders approved Paul's Gospel.
They added nothing to it (Gal. 2:6b) and thereby
declared the Judaizers to be wrong. But this private meeting was only the beginning.

Act 2—The Public Convocation (2:3-5)
The historical account of the Council of Jerusalem
is recorded by Luke (Acts 15:6-21). Several witnesses presented the case for the Gospel of the
grace of God, beginning with Peter (Acts 15:7-11).

It was he who had been chosen by God to take the Gospel to the Gentiles originally (Acts 10); and he reminds the assembly that God gave the Holy Spirit to the believing Gentiles just as He did to the Jews, so that there was "no difference."

This had been a difficult lesson for the early Christians to learn, because for centuries there had been a difference between Jews and Gentiles (Lev. 11:43-47; 20:22-27). In His death on the cross, Jesus had broken down the barriers between Jews and Gentiles (Eph. 2:11-22), so that in Christ there are no racial differences (Gal. 3:28). In his speech to the conference, Peter makes it clear that there is but one way of salvation: faith in Jesus Christ.

Then Paul and Barnabas told the assembly what God had done among the Gentiles (Acts 15:12), and what a "missionary report" that must have been! The "false brethren" who were there must have debated with Paul and Barnabas, but the two soldiers of the cross would not yield. Paul wanted the "truth of the Gospel" to continue among the Gentiles (Gal. 2:5).

It seems that Titus became a "test case" at this point. He was a Gentile Christian who had never submitted to circumcision. Yet it was clear to all that he was genuinely saved. Now, if the Judaizers were right ("Except you be circumcised after the manner of Moses, you cannot be saved," Acts 15:1), *then Titus was not a saved man.* But he *was* a saved man, and gave evidence of having the Holy Spirit; therefore, the Judaizers were wrong.

At this point, it might be helpful if we considered another associate of Paul—Timothy (see Acts 16:1-3). Was Paul being inconsistent by refusing to circumcise Titus, yet agreeing to circumcise Timothy? No, because two different issues were involved. In the case of Timothy, Paul was not submitting to Jewish law in order to win him to Christ. Timothy was part Jew, part Gentile, and his lack of circumcision would have hindered his ministry among the people of Israel. Titus was a full Gentile, and for him to have submitted would have indicated that he was missing something in his Christian experience. To have circumcised Titus would have been cowardice and compromise; *not* to have circumcised Timothy would have been to create unnecessary problems in his ministry.

James, the leader of the church, gave the summation of the arguments and the conclusion of the matter (Acts 15:13-21). As Jewish as he was, he made it clear that a Gentile does *not* have to become a Jew in order to become a Christian. God's program for this day is to "take out of the Gentiles a people for His name." Jews and Gentiles are saved the same way: through faith in Jesus Christ. James then asked that the assembly counsel the Gentiles to do nothing that would offend unbelieving Jews, lest they hinder them from being saved. Paul won the battle.

His view prevailed in the private meeting when the leaders approved his Gospel and in the public meeting when the group agreed with Paul and opposed the Judaizers.

Echoes of the Jerusalem conference are heard repeatedly in Paul's letter to the Galatians. Paul mentions the "yoke of bondage" (5:1), reminding us of Peter's similar warning (Acts 15:10). The themes of liberty and bondage are repeated often (Gal. 2:4; 4:3, 9, 21-31; 5:1), as is the idea of circumcision (2:3; 5:3-4; 6:12-13).

Centuries later, today's Christians need to appreciate afresh the courageous stand Paul and his associates took for the liberty of the Gospel. Paul's concern was "the truth of the Gospel" (2:5, 14), not the "peace of the church." The wisdom that God sends from above is "first pure, then peaceable" (James 3:17). "Peace at any price" was not Paul's philosophy of ministry, nor should it be ours.

Ever since Paul's time, the enemies of grace have been trying to add something to the simple Gospel of the grace of God. They tell us that a man is saved by faith in Christ *plus* something—good works, the Ten Commandments, baptism, church membership, religious ritual—and Paul makes it clear that these teachers are wrong. In fact, Paul pronounces a curse upon any person (man or angel) who preaches any other gospel than the Gospel of the grace of God, centered in Jesus Christ (Gal. 1:6-9; see 1 Cor. 15:1-7 for a definition of the Gospel). It is a serious thing to tamper with the Gospel.

Act 3—The Personal Confirmation (2:6-10)
The Judaizers had hoped to get the leaders of the Jerusalem church to disagree with Paul. By contrast, Paul makes it clear that he himself was not impressed either by the persons or the positions of the church leaders. He respected them, of course. Otherwise he would not have consulted with them privately. But he did not fear them or seek to buy their influence. All he wanted them to do was recognize "the grace of God" at work in his life and ministry (Gal. 2:9), and this they did.

Not only did the assembly approve Paul's Gospel, and oppose Paul's enemies, but they encouraged Paul's ministry and recognized publicly that God had committed the Gentile aspect of His work into

Paul's hands. They could add nothing to Paul's message or ministry, and they dared not take anything away. There was agreement and unity: one Gospel would be preached to Jews and to Gentiles.

However, the leaders recognized, too, that God had assigned different areas of ministry to different men. Apart from his visit to the household of Cornelius (Acts 10) and to the Samaritans (Acts 8), Peter had centered his ministry primarily among the Jews. Paul had been called as God's special ambassador to the Gentiles. So, it was agreed that each man would minister in the sphere assigned to him by God.

"The Gospel of the circumcision" and "the Gospel of the uncircumcision" are not two different messages; it had already been agreed that there is only one Gospel. Rather, we have here two different spheres of ministry, one to the Jews and the other to the Gentiles. Peter and Paul would both preach the same Gospel, and the same Lord would be at work in and through them (Gal. 2:8), but they would minister to different peoples.

This does not mean that Paul would never seek to win the Jews. To the contrary, he had a great burden on his heart for his people (Rom. 9:1-3). In fact, when Paul came to a city, he would first go to the Jewish synagogue, if there was one, and start his work among his own people. Nor was Peter excluded from ministering to the Gentiles. But each man would concentrate his work in his own sphere assigned to him by the Holy Spirit. James, Peter, and John would go to the Jews; Paul would go the Gentiles (Gal. 2:9b, where the word *heathen* means "Gentile nations").

The Jerusalem conference began with a great possibility for division and dissension; yet it ended with cooperation and agreement. "Behold, how good and how pleasant it is for brethren to dwell together in unity" (Ps. 133:1). Perhaps we need to practice some of this same cooperation today.

We need to recognize the fact that God calls people to different ministries in different places; yet we all preach the same Gospel and are seeking to work together to build His church. Among those who know and love Christ, there can be no such thing as "competition." Peter was a great man, and perhaps the leading apostle; yet he gladly yielded to Paul—a newcomer—and permitted him to carry on his ministry as the Lord led him. Previously, Paul explained his *independence* from the apostles (Gal. 1); now in chapter 2 he points out his *interdependence* with the apostles. He was free, and yet he was willingly in fellowship with them in the ministry of the Gospel.

We move next from the theological to the practical—helping the poor (v. 10). Certainly these things go together. Correct doctrine is never a substitute for Christian duty (James 2:14-26). Too often our church meetings discuss problems, but they fail to result in practical help for the needy world. Paul had always been interested in the poor (Acts 11:27-30), so he was glad to follow their suggestion.

Even though the conference ended with Paul and the leaders in agreement, it did not permanently solve the problem. The Judaizers did not give up, but persisted in interfering with Paul's work and invading the churches he founded. Paul carried the good news of the council's decision to the churches in Antioch, Syria, and Cilicia (Acts 15:23) and in the other areas where he had ministered (Acts 16:4). But the Judaizers followed at his heels (like yelping dogs—see Phil. 3:1-3), starting at Antioch where they even swayed Peter to their cause (see Gal. 2:11 ff.).

There is little question that the Judaizers went to the churches of Galatia to sow their seeds of discord, and for this reason Paul had to write the letter we are now studying. It may have been written from Antioch shortly after the Council of Jerusalem, though some scholars date it later and have Paul writing from either Ephesus or Corinth. These historical details are important, but they are not vital to an understanding of the letter itself. Suffice it to say that this is probably Paul's earliest letter, and in it we find every major doctrine that Paul believed, preached, and wrote about in his subsequent ministry.

The curtain falls on this drama, but it will go up to reveal another. Once again God's "freedom fighter" will have to defend the truth of the Gospel, this time before Peter.

But when Peter was come to Antioch, I withstood him to the face, because he was to be blamed. For before that certain came from James, he did eat with the Gentiles; but when they were come, he withdrew and separated himself, fearing them which were of the circumcision. And the other Jews dissembled likewise with him; insomuch that Barnabas also was carried away with their dissimulation.

But when I saw that they walked not uprightly according to the truth of the Gospel, I said unto Peter before them all, "If thou, being a Jew, livest after the manner of Gentiles, and not as do the Jews, why compellest thou the Gentiles to live as do the Jews? We who are Jews by nature, and not sinners of the Gentiles, knowing that a man is not justified by the works of the law, but by the faith of Jesus Christ, even we have believed in Jesus Christ, that we might be justified by the faith of Christ, and not by the works of the law: for by the works of the law shall no flesh be justified.

"But if, while we seek to be justified by Christ, we ourselves also are found sinners, is therefore Christ the minister of sin? God forbid. For if I build again the things which I destroyed, I make myself a transgressor.

"For I through the law am dead to the law, that I might live unto God. I am crucified with Christ: nevertheless I live; yet not I, but Christ liveth in me: and the life which I now live in the flesh I live by the faith of the Son of God, who loved me, and gave Himself for me.

"I do not frustrate the grace of God: for if righteousness came by the law, then Christ is dead in vain."

4

The Freedom Fighter, Part II

"Eternal vigilance is the price of liberty!"

Wendell Phillips said that at a Massachusetts anti-slavery meeting in 1852, but its sentiment is valid today—not only in the realm of the political, but even more so in the realm of the spiritual. Paul had risked his life to carry the Gospel of God's grace to the regions beyond, and he was not willing for the enemy to rob him or his churches of their liberty in Christ. It was this "spiritual vigilance" that led Paul into another dramatic encounter, this time with the Apostle Peter, Barnabas, and some of the friends of James. Again, the drama is in three acts.

1. Peter's Relapse (2:11-13)

Apparently, sometime after the important conference described in Acts 15, Peter came from Jerusalem to Antioch. The first thing to note is *Peter's freedom* then. He enjoyed fellowship with *all* the believers, Jews and Gentiles alike. To "eat with the Gentiles" meant to accept them, to put Jews and Gentiles on the same level as one family in Christ.

Raised as an orthodox Jew, Peter had a difficult time learning this lesson. Jesus had taught it while He was with Peter before the crucifixion (Matt. 15:1-20). The Holy Spirit had reemphasized it when He sent Peter to the home of Cornelius, the Roman centurion (Acts 10). Furthermore, the truth had been accepted and approved by the conference of leaders at Jerusalem (Acts 15). Peter had been one of the key witnesses at that time.

But before we criticize Peter, perhaps we had better examine our own lives to see how many familiar Bible doctrines *we* are actually obeying. As you examine church history, you see that, even with a complete Bible, believers through the years have been slow to believe and practice the truths of the Christian faith. When we think of the persecution and discrimination that have been practiced in the name of Christ, it embarrasses us. It is one thing for us to defend a doctrine in a church meeting, and quite something else to put it into practice in everyday life.

Peter's freedom was threatened by *Peter's fear*. While he was in Antioch, the church was visited by some of the associates of James. (You will remember that James was a strict Jew even though he was a Christian believer.) Paul does not suggest that James sent these men to investigate Peter, or even that they were officials of the Jerusalem church. No doubt they belonged to the "circumcision party" (Acts 15:1, 5) and wanted to lead the Antioch church into religious legalism.

After his experience with Cornelius, Peter had been "called on the carpet" and had ably defended himself (Acts 11). But now, he became afraid. Peter had not been afraid to obey the Spirit when He sent him to Cornelius, nor was he afraid to give his witness at the Jerusalem conference. But now, with the arrival of some members of "the opposition," Peter lost his courage. "The fear of man bringeth a snare" (Prov. 29:25).

How do we account for this fear? For one thing, we know that Peter was an impulsive man. He could show amazing faith and courage one minute and fail completely the next. He walked on the waves to go to Jesus, but then became frightened and began to sink. He boasted in the upper room that he would willingly die with Jesus, and then denied his Lord three times. Peter in the Book of Acts is certainly more consistent than in the four Gospels, but he was not perfect—*nor are we!* Peter's fear led to *Peter's fall.* He ceased to enjoy the "love feast" with the Gentile believers and separated himself from them.

There are two tragedies to Peter's fall. First, it made him a hypocrite (which is the meaning of the word *dissembled*). Peter pretended that his actions were motivated by faithfulness, when they were really motivated by fear. How easy it is to use "Bible doctrine" to cover up our disobedience.

The second tragedy is that *Peter led others astray with him.* Even Barnabas was involved. Barnabas had been one of the spiritual leaders of the church in Antioch (Acts 11:19-26), so his disobedience would have a tremendous influence on the others in the fellowship.

Suppose Peter and Barnabas had won the day and led the church into legalism? What might the results have been? Would Antioch have continued to be the great missionary church that sent out Paul and Barnabas? (Acts 13) Would they, instead, have sent out the "missionaries" of the circumcision party and either captured or divided the churches Paul had already founded? You can see that this problem was not a matter of personality or party; it was a question of "the truth of the Gospel." And Paul was prepared to fight for it.

2. Paul's Rebuke (2:14-21)

Bible students are not sure just where Paul's conversation with Peter ends and where his letter to the Galatians continues in the passage. It does not really matter since the entire section deals with the same topic: our liberty in Jesus Christ. We will assume that the entire section represents Paul's rebuke of Peter, even though it may be in a condensed form. It is interesting to note that Paul builds the entire rebuke on *doctrine*. There are five basic Christian doctrines that were being denied by Peter because of his separation from the Gentiles.

(1) *The unity of the church* (2:14). Peter was a Jew, but through his faith in Christ he had become a Christian. Because he was a Christian, he was part of the church, and in the church there are no racial distinctions (Gal. 3:28). We have seen how the Lord taught Peter this important lesson, first in the house of Cornelius and then at the Jerusalem conference.

Paul's words must have stung Peter: "You are a Jew, yet you have been living like a Gentile. Now you want the Gentiles to live like Jews. What kind of inconsistency is that?"

Peter himself had stated at the Jerusalem conference that God had "put no difference between us and them" (Acts 15:9). But now *Peter* was putting a difference. God's people are one people, even though they may be divided into various groups. Any practice on our part that violates the

Scripture and separates brother from brother is a denial of the unity of the body of Christ.

(2) *Justification by faith* (2:15-16). This is the first appearance of the important word *justification* in this letter, and probably in Paul's writings (if, as we believe, Galatians was the first letter he wrote). "Justification by faith" was the watchword of the Reformation, and it is important that we understand this doctrine.

"How should [a] man be just with God?" (Job 9:2) was a vital question, because the answer determined eternal consequences. "The just shall live by his faith" (Hab. 2:4) is God's answer; and it was this truth that liberated Martin Luther from religious bondage and fear. So important is this concept that three New Testament books explain it to us: Romans (see 1:17), Galatians (see 3:11), and Hebrews (see 10:38). Romans explains the meaning of "the just"; Galatians explains "shall live"; and Hebrews explains "by faith."

But what is justification? *Justification is the act of God whereby He declares the believing sinner righteous in Jesus Christ.* Every word of this definition is important. Justification is *an act* and not a process. No Christian is "more justified" than another Christian. "Having therefore been once-and-for-all justified by faith, we have peace with God" (Rom. 5:1, literal translation). Since we are justified by faith, it is an instant and immediate transaction between the believing sinner and God. If we were justified by works, then it would have to be a gradual process.

Furthermore, justification is an act *of God;* it is not the result of man's character or works. "It is God that justifieth" (Rom. 8:33). It is not by doing the "works of the law" that the sinner gets a right standing before God, but by putting his faith in Jesus Christ. As Paul will explain later in this letter, the law was given to reveal sin and not to redeem from sin (see Rom. 3:20). God in His grace has put our sins on Christ—and Christ's righteousness has been put to our account (see 2 Cor. 5:21).

In justification, God *declares* the believing sinner righteous; He does not *make* him righteous. (Of course, real justification leads to a changed life, which is what James 2 is all about.) Before the sinner trusts Christ, he stands GUILTY before God; but the moment he trusts Christ, he is declared NOT GUILTY and he can never be called GUILTY again!

Justification is not simply "forgiveness," because a person could be forgiven and then go out and sin and become guilty. Once you have been "justified by faith" you can never be held guilty before God.

Justification is also different from "pardon," because a pardoned criminal still has a record. When the sinner is justified by faith, *his past sins are remembered against him no more,* and God no longer puts his sins on record (see Ps. 32:1-2; Rom. 4:1-8).

Finally, God justifies *sinners,* not "good people." Paul declares that God justifies "the ungodly" (Rom. 4:5). The reason most sinners are not justified is because they will not admit they are sinners! And sinners are the only kind of people Jesus Christ can save (Matt. 9:9-13; Luke 18:9-14).

When Peter separated himself from the Gentiles, he was denying the truth of justification by faith, because he was saying, "We Jews are different from—and better than—the Gentiles." Yet both Jews and Gentiles are sinners (Rom. 3:22-23) and can be saved only by faith in Christ.

(3) *Freedom from the law* (2:17-18). At the Jerusalem conference, Peter had compared the Mosaic law to a burdensome yoke (Acts 15:10; see Gal. 5:1). Now he had put himself under that impossible yoke.

Paul's argument goes like this: "Peter, you and I did not find salvation through the law; we found it through faith in Christ. But now, after being saved, you go back into the law! This means that Christ alone did not save you; otherwise you would not have needed the law. So, Christ actually made you a sinner!

"Furthermore, you have preached the Gospel of God's grace to Jews and Gentiles, and have told them they are saved by faith and not by keeping the law. By going back into legalism, you are building up what you tore down! This means that you sinned by tearing it down to begin with!"

In other words, Paul is arguing from Peter's own experience of the grace of God. To go back to Moses is to deny everything that God had done for him and through him.

(4) *The very Gospel itself* (2:19-20). If a man is justified by the works of the law, then why did Jesus Christ die? His death, burial, and resurrection are the key truths of the Gospel (1 Cor. 15: 1-8). We are *saved* by faith in Christ (He died for us), and we *live* by faith in Christ (He lives in us). Furthermore, we are so identified with Christ by the Spirit that *we died with Him* (see Rom. 6). This means that we are dead to the law. To go back to Moses is to return to the graveyard! We have been "raised to walk in newness of life" (Rom. 6:4); and since we live by His resurrection power, we do not need the "help" of the law.

(5) *The grace of God* (2:21). The Judaizers

wanted to mix law and grace, but Paul tells us that this is impossible. To go back to the law means to "set aside" the grace of God.

Peter had experienced God's grace in his own salvation, and he had proclaimed God's grace in his own ministry. But when he withdrew from the Gentile Christian fellowship, he openly denied the grace of God.

Grace says, "There is no difference! All are sinners, and all can be saved through faith in Christ!"

But Peter's actions had said, "There *is* a difference! The grace of God is not sufficient; we also need the law."

Returning to the law nullifies the cross: "If righteousness came by the law, then Christ is dead in vain" (v. 21). Law says DO! Grace says DONE! "It is finished!" was Christ's victory cry (John 19:30). "For by grace are ye saved through faith" (Eph. 2:8).

We have no record of Peter's reply to Paul's rebuke, but Scripture would indicate that he admitted his sin and was restored to the fellowship once again. Certainly when you read his two letters (1 and 2 Peter), you detect no deviation from the Gospel of the grace of God. In fact, the theme of 1 Peter is "the true grace of God" (5:12); and the word *grace* is used in every chapter of the letter. Peter is careful to point out that he and Paul were in complete agreement, lest anyone try to "rob Peter to pay Paul" (2 Peter 3:15-16).

So end the two acts of this exciting drama. But the curtain has not come down yet, for there is a third act which involves you and me.

3. The Believer's Response

We know what Peter's response was when he was

challenged to live up to the truth of the Gospel: fear and failure. And we know what Paul's response was when he saw the truth of the Gospel being diluted: courage and defense. But the important question *today* is: what is *my* response to the "truth of the Gospel"? Perhaps this is a good place to take inventory of ourselves before we proceed into the doctrinal chapters of this letter. Let me suggest some questions for each of us to answer.

(1) *Have I been saved by the grace of God?* The only Gospel that saves is the Gospel of the grace of God as revealed in Jesus Christ. Any other Gospel is a false gospel and is under a curse (Gal. 1:6-9). Someone has defined "grace" as

God's
Riches
At
Christ's
Expense,

and a good definition it is. Am I trusting in *myself* for salvation—*my* morality, *my* good works, even *my* religion? If so, then I am not a Christian, for a true Christian is one who has trusted Christ *alone*. "For by grace are ye saved through faith; and that not of yourselves: it is the gift of God: not of works, lest any man should boast" (Eph. 2:8-9).

(2) *Am I trying to mix law and grace?* Law means I must do something to please God, while grace means that God has finished the work for me and all I need do is believe on Christ. Salvation is not by faith in Christ *plus* something: it is by faith in Christ *alone*. While church membership and religious activities are good in their place as expressions of faith in Christ, they can never be added to faith in Christ in order to secure eternal life. "And if by grace, then is it no more of works:

otherwise grace is no more grace. But if it be of works, then it is no more grace: otherwise work is no more work" (Rom. 11:6).

(3) *Am I rejoicing in the fact that I am justified by faith in Christ?* It has often been said that "justified" means "just as if I'd never sinned" and this is correct. It brings great peace to the heart to know that one has a right standing before God (Rom. 5:1). Just think: the righteousness of Christ has been put to our account! God has not only declared that we are righteous in Christ, but He deals with us as though we had never sinned at all! We need never fear judgment because our sins have already been judged in Christ on the cross (Rom. 8:1).

(4) *Am I walking in the liberty of grace?* Liberty does not mean license; rather, it means the freedom in Christ to enjoy Him and to become what He has determined for us to become (Eph. 2:10). It is not only "freedom to *do*" but also "freedom *not* to do." We are no longer in bondage to sin and the law. As Paul will explain in the practical section of this letter (chaps. 5 and 6), we obey God because of love and not because of law. Christians enjoy a wonderful liberty in Christ. Am I enjoying it?

(5) *Am I willing to defend the truth of the Gospel?* This does not mean that we become evangelical detectives investigating every church and Sunday School class in town. But it does mean that we do not fear men when they deny the truths that have brought us eternal life in Christ. "Do I seek to please men? For if I yet pleased men, I should not be the servant of Christ" (Gal. 1:10).

Many people with whom we come in contact actually believe that people are saved by faith in Christ plus "doing good works . . . keeping the

Ten Commandments . . . obeying the Sermon on the Mount," and any number of other "religious *pluses.*" We may not have the same apostolic authority that Paul exercised, but we do have the Word of God to proclaim; and it is our obligation to share the truth.

(6) *Am I "walking uprightly according to the truth of the Gospel"?* (Gal. 2:14) The best way to defend the truth is to live the truth. My verbal defense of the Gospel will accomplish very little if my life contradicts what I say. Paul is going to explain to us how to live in liberty by the grace of God, and it is important that we obey what he says.

A new employee was instructed how to measure valve parts to make sure they were ready for the final assembly. But after a few hours, his foreman was receiving complaints that the parts he was approving were faulty. "What are you doing?" the foreman asked. "I showed you how to use that micrometer. You're sending through parts that are oversize!"

The employee replied, "Oh, most of the parts I was measuring were too large, so I opened up the micrometer a bit."

Changing the standards will never make for success, either in manufacturing or ministry. Paul maintained the standards of "the truth of the Gospel" —and so should we.

Part II

Doctrinal Section:

Grace
and the Law

Chapters 3—4

O foolish Galatians, who hath bewitched you, that ye should not obey the truth, before whose eyes Jesus Christ hath been evidently set forth, crucified among you? This only would I learn of you, received ye the Spirit by the works of the law, or by the hearing of faith? Are ye so foolish? having begun in the Spirit, are ye now made perfect by the flesh? Have ye suffered so many things in vain? If it be yet in vain. He therefore that ministereth to you the Spirit, and worketh miracles among you, doeth he it by the works of the law, or by the hearing of faith?

Even as Abraham believed God, and it was accounted to him for righteousness. Know ye therefore that they which are of faith, the same are the children of Abraham.

And the Scripture, foreseeing that God would justify the heathen through faith, preached before the Gospel unto Abraham, saying, "In thee shall all nations be blessed." So then they which be of faith are blessed with faithful Abraham.

For as many as are of the works of the law are under the curse: for it is written, "Cursed is every one that continueth not in all things which are written in the book of the law to do them."

But that no man is justified by the law in the sight of God, it is evident: for, "The just shall live by faith." And the law is not of faith: but, "The man that doeth them shall live in them."

Christ hath redeemed us from the curse of the law, being made a curse for us: for it is written, "Cursed is every one that hangeth on a tree," that the blessing of Abraham might come on the Gentiles through Jesus Christ; that we might receive the promise of the Spirit through faith.

5

Bewitched
and Bothered

The 60 verses that make up Galatians 3 and 4 are some of the strongest writing that Paul ever penned. But, after all, he was in a battle! He was out to prove that salvation is by grace alone, and not by the works of the law. His opponents had used every possible means to try to capture the churches of Galatia, and Paul was not going to fight them half-heartedly. The apostle was no amateur when it came to debate, and in these two chapters he certainly proves his abilities. His logic is unassailable.

Paul uses six different arguments to prove that God saves sinners through faith in Christ and not by the works of the law. He begins with the *personal argument* (3:1-5) in which he asks the Galatians to recall their personal experience with Christ when they were saved. Then he moves into the *scriptural argument* (3:6-14), in which he quotes six Old Testament passages to prove his point. In the *logical argument* (3:15-29) he reasons with his readers on the basis of what a covenant is and how a covenant works. He then presents the *historical argument* (4:1-11), explaining the place of law in the history of Israel.

At this point, Paul's love for his converts comes to the surface. The result is a *sentimental argument* (4:12-18) as the apostle appeals to them to remember his love and their happy relationship in days past. But then Paul goes right back to his close reasoning, and concludes with the *allegorical argument* (4:19-31), based on the life of Abraham and his relationships with Sarah and Hagar. Practical application of his doctrinal argument follows in the last two chapters.

1. The Personal Argument (3:1-5)

The key to this section is in the word *suffered* (v. 4), which can be translated "experienced." Paul asks, "Have you experienced so many things in vain?" The argument from Christian experience was a wise one with which to begin, because Paul had been with them when they had trusted Christ. Of course, to argue from experience can be dangerous, because experiences can be counterfeited and they can be misunderstood. Subjective experience must be balanced with objective evidence, because experiences can change, but truth never changes. Paul balances the subjective experience of the Galatian Christians with the objective teaching of the unchanging Word of God (vv. 6-14).

It was obvious that these people had experienced something in their lives when Paul had first visited them; but the Judaizers had come along and convinced them that their experience was not complete. They needed something else, and that "something else" was obedience to the law of Moses. These false teachers had bewitched them and turned them into fools. In calling them "fools"

Paul is not violating Christ's words in the Sermon on the Mount (Matt. 5:22), because two different words are used and two different ideas are expressed. *Foolish* in Galatians 3:1 means "spiritually dull" (see Luke 24:25), while the word Jesus used carries the idea of "a godless person." Paul is declaring a fact; Jesus is warning against verbal abuse.

Paul reminds them that they had truly experienced a meeting with God.

They saw God the Son (3:1). It was "Christ and Him crucified" that Paul had preached in Galatia, and with such effectiveness that the people could almost see Jesus crucified for them on the cross. The words *evidently set forth* translate a Greek word that means "publicly portrayed, or announced on a poster." Just as we put important information on a poster and display it in a public place, so Paul openly presented Christ to the Galatians, with great emphasis on His death for sinners on the cross. They heard this truth, believed it, and obeyed it; and as a result, were born into the family of God.

They received God the Holy Spirit (3:2-3). The Holy Spirit is mentioned 18 times in this epistle and plays an important part in Paul's defense of the Gospel of the grace of God. The only real evidence of conversion is the presence of the Holy Spirit in the life of the believer (see Rom. 8:9). Paul asks an important question: did they receive the Spirit by faith in the Word of God, or by doing the works of the law? Of course, there could be but one answer: the Spirit came into their lives because they trusted Jesus Christ.

It is important that we understand the work of the Spirit in salvation and Christian living. The Holy Spirit *convicts* the lost sinner and reveals Christ to him (John 16:7-11). The sinner can resist the Spirit (Acts 7:51) or yield to the Spirit and trust Jesus Christ. When the sinner believes in Christ, he is then *born of the Spirit* (John 3:1-8) and receives new life. He is also *baptized by the Spirit* so that he becomes a part of the spiritual body of Christ (1 Cor. 12:12-14). The believer is *sealed by the Spirit* (Eph. 1:13-14) as a guarantee that he will one day share in the glory of Christ.

Since the Holy Spirit does so much for the believer, this means that the believer has a responsibility to the Holy Spirit, who lives within his body (1 Cor. 6:19-20). The Christian should *walk in the Spirit* (Gal. 5:16, 25) by reading the Word, praying, and obeying God's will. If he disobeys God, then he is *grieving the Spirit* (Eph. 4:30), and if he persists in doing this, he may *quench the Spirit* (1 Thes. 5:19). This does not mean that the Holy Spirit will leave him, because Jesus has promised that the Spirit abides forever (John 14:16). But it does mean that the Spirit cannot give him the joy and power that he needs for daily Christian living. Believers should be *filled with the Spirit* (Eph. 5:18-21), which simply means "controlled by the Spirit." This is a continuous experience, like drinking water from a fresh stream (John 7:37-39).

So, in their conversion experience, the believers in Galatia had received the Spirit by faith and not by the works of the law. This leads Paul to another question: "If you did not *begin* with the law, why bring it in anyway? If you began with the Spirit, can you go on to maturity without the Spirit, depending on the flesh?" The word *flesh* here does not refer to the human body, but rather to the believer's old nature. Whatever the Bible says about "flesh" is usually negative (see Gen. 6:1-7; Rom. 7:18; John 6:63; Phil. 3:3). Since we were saved through the Spirit, and not the flesh, through faith and not law, then it is reasonable that we should continue that way.

The illustration of human birth is appropriate here. Two human parents are required for a child to be conceived and born, and two *spiritual* parents are required for a child to be born into God's family: the Spirit of God and the Word of God (John 3:1-8; 1 Peter 1:22-25). When a normal child is born, he has all that he needs for life; nothing need be added. When the child of God is born into God's family, he has all that he needs spiritually; *nothing need be added!* All that is necessary is that the child have food, exercise, and cleansing that he might grow into maturity. It would be strange if the parents had to take the child to the doctor at one month to receive ears, at two months to receive toes, and so on.

"You have begun in the Spirit," writes Paul. "Nothing need be added! Walk in the Spirit and you will grow in the Lord."

They experienced miracles from God the Father (3:5). The *He* in this verse refers to the Father as the One who ministers the Spirit and "worketh miracles among [them]." The same Holy Spirit who came into the believer at conversion continues to work in him and through him so that the whole body is built up (see Col. 2:19; Eph. 4:16). The Father continues to supply the Spirit in power and blessing, and this is done by faith and not by the works of the law. The phrase *among you* can also be translated *within you.* These miracles would therefore include wonderful changes *within* the lives of the Christians, as well as signs and wonders within the church fellowship.

"Do you really believe the miracles in the Bible?"

a skeptic asked a new Christian who had been a terrible drinker.

"Of course I do!" the believer replied.

The skeptic laughed. "Do you mean that you really believe that Jesus could turn water into wine?" he asked.

"I sure do! In my home He turned wine into food and clothing and furniture."

2. The Scriptural Argument (3:6-14)

Paul turns now from subjective experience to the objective evidence of the Word of God. We never judge the Scriptures by our experience; we test our experience by the Word of God. In the first section, Paul asked six questions; in this section he will quote six Old Testament statements to prove that salvation is by faith in Christ and not by the works of the law. Since the Judaizers wanted to take the believers back into the law, Paul quotes the law! And, since they magnified the place of Abraham in their religion, Paul uses Abraham as one of his witnesses!

(1) *Abraham was saved by faith* (3:6-7). Paul begins by quoting Moses to show that God's righteousness was placed to Abraham's account only because he believed God's promise (Gen. 15:6). The words *accounted* in Galatians 3:6 and *counted* in Genesis 15:6 mean the same as *imputed* in Romans 4:11, 22-24. The Greek word means "to put to one's account." When the sinner trusts Christ, God's righteousness is put to his account. More than this, the believer's sins are no longer put to his account (see Rom. 4:1-8). This means that the record is always clean before God, and therefore the believer can never be brought into judgment for his sins.

The Jewish people were very proud of their relationship with Abraham. The trouble was, they thought that this relationship guaranteed them eternal salvation. John the Baptist warned them that their *physical* descent did not guarantee *spiritual* life (Matt. 3:9). Jesus made a clear distinction between "Abraham's seed" physically and "Abraham's children" spiritually (John 8:33-47). Some people today still imagine that salvation is inherited. Because mother and father were godly people, the children are automatically saved. But this is not true. It has well been said, "God has no grandchildren."

(2) *This salvation is for the Gentiles* (3:8-9). The word *heathen* (v. 8), as used here, simply means Gentiles. Paul's quotation of Moses (Gen. 12:3) proves that, from the very beginning of Abraham's relationship with God, the blessing of salvation was promised to all the nations of the world. God preached the "Good News" to Abraham centuries ago, and Paul brought that same Good News to the Galatians: sinners are justified through faith and not by keeping the law. The logic here is evident: if God promised to save the Gentiles by faith, then the Judaizers are wrong in wanting to take the Gentile believers back into law. The true "children of Abraham" are not the Jews by physical descent, but Jews and Gentiles who have believed in Jesus Christ. All those who are "of faith" (believers) are blessed with "believing Abraham."

When you read God's great covenant with Abraham in Genesis 12:1-3, you discover that many different blessings were promised—some personal, some national and political, and some universal and spiritual. Certainly God did make Abraham's name great; he is revered not only by Jews, but also by Christians, Muslims, and many others. God did multiply his descendants, and God did bless those who blessed Abraham. He also judged those who cursed his descendants (Egypt, Babylon, and Rome are cases in point). But the greatest blessings that God sent through Abraham and the Jewish nation have to do with our eternal salvation. Jesus Christ is that promised "Seed," through whom all the nations have been blessed (Gal. 3:16).

(3) *This salvation is by faith, not law* (3:10-12). Salvation could never come by obedience to law because the law brings a curse, not a blessing. Here Paul quotes from Deuteronomy (27:26). Law demands obedience, and this means obedience in *all things*. The law is not a "religious cafeteria" where people can pick and choose (see James 2:10-11). Paul next quotes Habakkuk, "The just shall live by his faith" (2:4). This statement is so important that the Holy Spirit inspired three New Testament books to explain it as mentioned before. *Romans* explains "the just" and tells how the sinner can be justified before God (see Rom. 1:17). *Galatians* explains how the just "shall live"; and *Hebrews* discusses "by faith" (see Heb. 10:38). Nobody could ever live "by law" because the law kills and shows the sinner he is guilty before God (Romans 3:20; 7:7-11).

But someone might argue that it takes faith even to obey the law; so Paul quotes Leviticus to prove that it is *doing* the law, not believing it, that God requires (18:5). Law says, "Do and live!" but grace says, "Believe and live!" Paul's own experience (Phil. 3:1-10), as well as the history of Israel (Rom. 10:1-10), proves that works righteousness can never save the sinner; only faith righteousness can do that.

The Judaizers wanted to seduce the Galatians into a religion of legal works, while Paul wanted them to enjoy a relationship of love and life by faith in Christ. For the Christian to abandon faith and grace for law and works is to lose everything exciting that the Christian can experience in his daily fellowship with the Lord. The law cannot justify the sinner (Gal. 2:16); neither can it give him righteousness (2:21). The law cannot give the gift of the Spirit (3:2), nor can it guarantee that spiritual inheritance that belongs to God's children (3:18). The law cannot give life (3:21), and the law cannot give liberty (4:8-10). Why, then, go back into the law?

(4) *This salvation comes through Christ* (3:13-14). These two verses beautifully summarize all that Paul has been saying in this section. Does the law put sinners under a curse? Then Christ has redeemed us from that curse! Do you want the blessing of Abraham? It comes through Christ! Do you want the gift of the Spirit, but you are a Gentile? This gift is given through Christ to the Gentiles! All that you need is in Christ! There is no reason to go back to Moses.

Paul quotes Deuteronomy again, "He that is hanged is accursed of God" (21:33). The Jews did not crucify criminals; they stoned them to death. But in cases of shameful violation of the law, the body was hung on a tree and exposed for all to see. This was a great humiliation, because the Jewish people were very careful in their treatment of a dead body. After the body had been exposed for a time, it was taken down and buried (see Josh. 8:29; 10:26; 2 Sam. 4:12).

Of course, Paul's reference to a "tree" relates to the cross on which Jesus died (Acts 5:30; 1 Peter

2:24). He was not stoned and then His dead body
exposed; He was nailed alive to a tree and left there
to die. But by dying on the cross, Jesus Christ bore
the curse of the law for us; so that now the believer is no longer under the law and its awful
curse. "The blessing of Abraham" (justification by
faith and the gift of the Spirit) is now ours through
faith in Jesus Christ.

The word *redeemed* in verse 13 means to purchase a slave for the purpose of setting him free.
It is possible to purchase a slave and keep him as
a slave, but this is not what Christ did. By shedding
His blood on the cross, He purchased us that we
might be set free. The Judaizers wanted to lead
the Christians into slavery, but Christ died to set
them free. Salvation is not exchanging one form of
bondage for another. Salvation is being set free
from the bondage of sin and the law *into* the liberty of God's grace through Christ.

This raises an interesting question: how could
these Judaizers ever convince the Galatian Christians that the way of law was better than the way
of grace? Why would any believer deliberately
want to choose bondage instead of liberty? Perhaps
part of the answer is found in the word *bewitched*
that Paul uses in verse 1. The word means "to cast
a spell, to fascinate." What is there about legalism
that can so fascinate the Christian that he will turn
from grace to law?

For one thing, legalism appeals to the flesh. The
flesh loves to be "religious"—to obey laws, to observe holy occasions, even to fast (see Gal. 4:10).
Certainly there is nothing wrong with obedience,
fasting, or solemn times of spiritual worship,
*provided that the Holy Spirit does the motivating
and the empowering.* The flesh loves to boast about

its religious achievements—how many prayers were offered, or how many gifts were given (see Luke 18:9-14; Phil. 3:1-10).

Another characteristic of religious legalism that fascinates people is the appeal to the senses. Instead of worshiping God "in spirit and in truth" (John 4:24), the legalist invents his own system that satisfies his senses. He cannot walk by faith; he has to walk by sight, and hearing, and tasting, and smelling, and feeling. To be sure, true Spirit-led worship does not deny the five senses. We see other believers; we sing and hear the hymns; we taste and feel the elements of the Lord's Supper. But these external things are but windows through which faith perceives the eternal. They are not ends in themselves.

The person who depends on religion can measure himself and compare himself with others. This is another fascination to legalism. But the true believer measures himself with Christ, not other Christians (Eph. 4:11 ff.). There is no room for pride in the spiritual walk of the Christian who lives by grace; but the legalist constantly boasts about his achievements and his converts (Gal. 6:13-14).

Yes, there is a fascination to the law, but it is only bait that leads to a trap; and once the believer takes the bait, he finds himself in bondage. Far better to take God at His Word and rest on His grace. We were saved "by grace, through faith" and we must live "by grace, through faith." This is the way to blessing. The other way is the way to bondage.

Brethren, I speak after the manner of men; though it be but a man's covenant, yet if it be confirmed, no man disannulleth, or addeth thereto.

Now to Abraham and his seed were the promises made. He saith not, "And to seeds," as of many; but as of one, "And to thy seed," which is Christ. And this I say, that the covenant, that was confirmed before of God in Christ, the law, which was 430 years after, cannot disannul, that it should make the promise of none effect. For if the inheritance be of the law, it is no more of promise: but God gave it to Abraham by promise.

Wherefore then serveth the law? It was added because of transgressions, till the seed should come to whom the promise was made; and it was ordained by angels in the hand of a mediator. Now a mediator is not a mediator of one, but God is one.

Is the law then against the promises of God? God forbid: for if there had been a law given which could have given life, verily righteousness should have been by the law. But the Scripture hath concluded all under sin, that the promise by faith of Jesus Christ might be given to them that believe.

But before faith came, we kept under the law, shut up unto the faith which should afterwards be revealed. Wherefore the law was our schoolmaster to bring us to Christ, that we might be justified by faith. But after that faith is come, we are no longer under a schoolmaster. For ye are all the children of God by faith in Christ Jesus.

For as many of you as have been baptized into Christ have put on Christ. There is neither Jew nor Greek, there is neither bond nor free, there is neither male nor female: for ye are all one in Christ Jesus. And if ye be Christ's, then are ye Abraham's seed, and heirs according to the promise.

6

The Logic
of Law

The Judaizers had Paul in a corner. He had just
finished proving from the Old Testament that God's
plan of salvation left no room for the works of the
law. But the fact that Paul quoted six times from
the Old Testament raised a serious problem: If salvation does not involve the law, then why was
the law given in the first place? Paul quoted from
the law to prove the insignificance of the law. If the
law is not set aside, then his very arguments are
worthless, because they are taken from the law.

Our faith is a logical faith and can be defended
on rational grounds. While there are divine mysteries in the faith that no man can fully explain, there
are also divine reasons that any sincere person can
understand. Paul was trained as a Jewish rabbi and
was fully equipped to argue his case. In this section, he makes four statements that help us understand the relationship between *promise* and *law*.

1. The Law Cannot Change the Promise (3:15-18)
The word *promise* is used eight times in these
verses, referring to God's promise to Abraham that

in him all the nations of the earth would be blessed
(Gen. 12:1-3). This promise involved being justified by faith and having all the blessings of salvation (Gal. 3:6-9). It is obvious that the promise
to Abraham (and, through Christ, to us today),
given about 2000 B.C., preceded by centuries the
Law of Moses (about 1450 B.C.). The Judaizers im-
plied that the giving of the law *changed* that original covenant of promise. Paul argues that it did
not.

To begin with, once two parties conclude an
agreement, a third party cannot come along years
later and change that agreement. The only persons
who can change an original agreement are the persons who made it. To add anything to it or take
anything from it would be illegal.

If this is true among sinful men, how much more
does it apply to a holy God? Note that Abraham
did not make a covenant with God; *God made a
covenant with Abraham!* God did not lay down any
conditions for Abraham to meet. In fact, when the
covenant was ratified *Abraham was asleep!* (See
Gen. 15.) It was a covenant of grace: God made
promises to Abraham; Abraham did not make
promises to God.

But Paul reveals another wonderful truth: God
made this promise, not only to Abraham, but also
to Christ. "And to thy seed, which is Christ" (Gal.
3:16).

The Bible concept of "the seed" goes back to
Genesis 3:15, after the fall of man. God states that
there will be a conflict in the world between Satan's
seed (children of the world, see John 8:33-44) and
the woman's seed (God's children, and, ultimately,
God's Son). The Scriptures show this conflict: Cain
versus Abel (see 1 John 3:10-12); Israel versus the

nations; John the Baptist and Jesus versus the Pharisees (Matt. 3:7-9; Matt. 23:29-33); the true believer
versus the counterfeit (see the Parable of the Tares,
Matt. 13:24-30, 36-43). Satan's goal in the Old
Testament was to keep the Seed (Christ) from being born into the world, for Satan knew that God's
Son would one day crush his head.

In the final analysis, God made this covenant of
promise with Abraham *through Christ,* so that the
only two parties who can make any changes are
God the Father and God the Son. *Moses cannot
alter this covenant!* He can add nothing to it; he
can take nothing from it. The Judaizers wanted to
add to God's grace (as though anything could be
added to grace!) and take from God's promises.
They had no right to do this since they were not
parties in the original covenant.

The 430 years of verse 17 has puzzled Bible students for many years. From Abraham's call (Gen.
12) to Jacob's arrival in Egypt (Gen. 46) is 215
years. (This may be computed as follows: Abraham
was 75 years old when God called him and 100
when Isaac was born, Gen. 12:4; 21:5. This gives
us 25 years. Isaac was 60 when Jacob was born,
Gen. 25:26; and Jacob was 130 years old when he
arrived in Egypt, Gen. 47:9. Thus, $25 + 60 + 130 =$
215 years.) But Moses tells us that Israel sojourned
in Egypt 430 years (Ex. 12:40); so the total number of years from Abraham's call to the giving of
the law is 645 years, not 430. The length of the stay
in Egypt is recorded also in Genesis 15:13 and Acts
7:6, where the round figure of 400 years is used.

Several solutions have been offered to this puz-
zle, but perhaps the most satisfying is this: Paul is
counting from the time Jacob went into Egypt,
when God appeared to him and *reaffirmed* the

covenant (Gen. 46:1-4). The 430 years is the time from God's confirmation of His promise to Jacob until the giving of the law at Sinai.

Regardless of what solution to the dating question we may choose, the basic argument is clear: a law given centuries later cannot change a covenant made by other parties. But suppose the later revelation, such as the Law of Moses, was greater and more glorious than the earlier? What then? Paul makes a second statement.

2. The Law Is Not Greater Than the Promise (3:19-20)

The account of the giving of the law is impressive (Ex. 19). There were thunders and lightnings, and the people were trembling with fear. Even Moses was shaking in his sandals (Heb. 12:18-21). It was a dramatic event in comparison with the giving of the covenant to Abraham (Gen. 15), and, of course, the Judaizers were impressed with these emotional externals. But Paul points out that the law is inferior to the covenant of promise in two ways.

The law was temporary (3:19a). "It was added . . . until the seed should come." Now it is obvious that a temporary law cannot be greater than a permanent covenant. When you read God's covenant with Abraham, you find no "ifs" in His words. Nothing was conditional; all was of grace. But the blessings of the law were dependent upon the meeting of certain conditions. Furthermore, the law had a terminus point: "until the Seed [Christ] should come." With the death and resurrection of Christ, the law was done away and now its righteous demands are fulfilled in us through the Spirit (Rom. 7:4; 8:1-4).

The law required a mediator (3:19b-20). When

God gave the law to Israel, He did it by means of angels and through the mediation of Moses. Israel "received the law by the disposition of angels" (Acts 7:53). This means that the nation received the law third-hand: from God to angels to Moses. But when God made His covenant with Abraham, He did it personally, without a mediator. God was revealing to Abraham all that He would do for him and his descendants. A mediator stands between two parties and helps them to agree; but there was no need for a mediator in Abraham's case since God was entering into a covenant with him, not Abraham with God. "God is one" (Gal. 3:20), therefore there was no need for a go-between.

The Judaizers were impressed by the *incidentals* of the law—glory, thunder, lightning, angels, and other externals. But Paul looked beyond incidentals to the *essentials*. The law was temporary, and required a mediator. The covenant of promise was permanent, and no mediator was required. There could be but one conclusion: the covenant was greater than the law.

3. The Law Is Not Contrary to the Promise (3:21-26)

You can almost hear the Judaizers shouting the question in verse 21: "Is the law then *against* the promises of God?" Is God contradicting Himself? Does His right hand not know what His left hand is doing? As he replies to this question, Paul reveals his deep insight into the ways and purposes of God. He does not say that the law *contradicts* the promise, but rather that it *cooperates* with the promise in fulfilling the purposes of God. While *law* and *grace* seem to be contrary to one another, if you go deep enough, you will discover that they actually *com-*

plement one another. Why, then, was the law given?

(1) *The law was not given to provide life* (3:21). Certainly the law of Moses regulated the lives of the Jewish people, but it did not and could not provide *spiritual* life to the people. (Gal. 3:21 should be matched with 2:21.) If life and righteousness could have come through the law, then Jesus Christ would never have died on the cross. But Jesus did die; therefore, the law could never give the sinner life and righteousness. It was "worship of the law" that led Israel into a self-righteous religion of works, the result of which was the rejection of Christ (Rom. 9:30—10:13).

(2) *The law was given to reveal sin* (3:19a, 22). It is here that we see the way that law and grace cooperate in bringing the lost sinner to Jesus Christ. Law shows the sinner his guilt, and grace shows him the forgiveness he can have in Christ. The law is "holy, and just, and good" (Rom. 7:12), but we are unholy, unjust, and bad. The law does not *make* us sinners; it reveals to us that we already *are* sinners (see Rom. 3:20). The law is a mirror that helps us see our "dirty faces" (James 1:22-25) —*but you do not wash your face with the mirror!* It is grace that provides the cleansing through the blood of Jesus Christ (see 1 John 1:7b).

There is a lawful use of the law, and there is an unlawful use (1 Tim. 1:8-11). The lawful use is to reveal sin and cause men to see their need of a Saviour. The unlawful use is to try to achieve salvation by the keeping of the law. When people claim they are saved by "keeping the Ten Commandments," they are revealing their ignorance of the true meaning of the law. The law concludes "all [men] under sin" (Gal. 3:22), Jews and Gentiles alike. But since *all* are under sin, then *all* may be saved by grace! God does not have two ways of salvation; He has but one—faith in Jesus Christ.

(3) *The law was given to prepare the way for Christ* (3:23-26). Here Paul uses an illustration that was familiar to all his readers—the child guardian. In many Roman and Greek households, well-educated slaves took the children to and from school and watched over them during the day. Sometimes they would teach the children, sometimes they would protect and prohibit, and sometimes they would even discipline. This is what Paul means by *schoolmaster* (3:24); but please do not read into this word our modern idea of a schoolteacher. The transliteration of the Greek would give us our word *pedagogue*, which literally means "a child conductor."

By using this illustration, Paul is saying several things about the Jews and their law. First, he is saying that the Jews were not *born* through the law, but rather were *brought up* by the law. The slave was not the child's father; he was the child's guardian and disciplinarian. So, the law did not *give* life to Israel; it *regulated* life. The Judaizers taught that the law was necessary for life and righteousness, and Paul's argument shows their error.

But the second thing Paul says is even more important: *the work of the guardian was preparation for the child's maturity.* Once the child came of age, he no longer needed the guardian. So the law was a preparation for the nation of Israel until the coming of the promised Seed, Jesus Christ. The ultimate goal in God's program was His coming (v. 22), but "before this faith [Christ] came" (v. 23, NIV), the nation was "imprisoned by the law" (literal translation).

The law separated Israel from the Gentile nations (Eph. 2:12-18); it governed every aspect of their lives. During the centuries of Jewish history, the law was preparing for the coming of Christ. The *demands* of the law reminded the people that they needed a Saviour. The *types* and *symbols* in the law were pictures of the coming Messiah (see Luke 24:27).

A good example of this purpose of the law is in the account of the rich young ruler (Matt. 19: 16 ff.). This young man had everything anybody could desire, but he was not satisfied. He had tried to keep the commandments all his life, but still something was missing. *But these commandments brought him to Christ!* This is one of the purposes of the law, to create in lost sinners a sense of guilt and need. The sad thing is that the young man was not honest as he looked into the mirror of the law, for the last commandment ("Thou shalt not covet") escaped him; and he went away without eternal life.

The law has performed its purpose: the Saviour has come and the "guardian" is no longer needed. It is tragic that the nation of Israel did not recognize their Messiah when He appeared. God finally had to destroy the temple and scatter the nation, so that today it is impossible for a devoted Jew to practice the faith of his fathers. He has no altar, no priesthood, no sacrifice, no temple, no king (Hosea 3:4). All of these have been fulfilled in Christ, so that any man—Jew or Gentile—who trusts Christ becomes a child of God.

The law cannot change the promise, and the law is not greater than the promise. But the law is not contrary to the promise: they work together to bring sinners to the Saviour.

4. The Law Cannot Do What the Promise Can Do (3:27-29)

With the coming of Jesus Christ, the nation of Israel moved out of childhood into adulthood. The long period of preparation was over. While there was a certain amount of glory to the law, there was a greater glory in the gracious salvation of God as found in Christ. The law could reveal sin and, to a certain extent, control behavior, but the law could not do for the sinner what Jesus Christ can do.

To begin with, the law could never justify the guilty sinner. "I will not justify the wicked," said the Lord (Ex. 23:7); yet Paul states that God "justifies the ungodly" (Rom. 4:5). King Solomon, at the dedication of the temple, reminded God to condemn the wicked and justify the righteous (1 Kings 8:32); and this was a proper request in light of the holiness of God. The trouble is, nobody was righteous! It is only through faith in Jesus Christ that the sinner is justified—declared righteous—before God.

Furthermore, the law could never give a person a oneness with God; it separated man from God. There was a fence around the tabernacle and a veil between the Holy Place and the Holy of Holies.

Faith in Jesus baptizes us "into Christ" (Gal. 3:27). This baptism of the Spirit identifies the believer with Christ and makes him part of His Body (1 Cor. 12:12-14). Water baptism is an outward picture of this inner work of the Holy Spirit (see Acts 10:44-48).

The phrase *put on Christ* (Gal. 3:27) refers to a change of garments. The believer has laid aside the dirty garments of sin (Isa. 64:6) and, by faith, received the robes of righteousness in Christ (see Col. 3:8-15). But to the Galatians, this idea of

"changing clothes" would have an additional meaning. When the Roman child came of age, he took
off the childhood garments and put on the toga of
the adult citizen. The believer in Christ is not just
a "child of God" he is also a "son of God" (see Gal.
3:26, where *children* ought to be translated "adult
sons"). The believer has an adult status before
God—so why go back into the childhood of the
law?

"All one in Christ Jesus"—what a tremendous
claim! The law created differences and distinctions, not only between individuals and nations, but
also between various kinds of foods and animals.
Jesus Christ came, not to divide, but to unite.

This must have been glorious news for the Galatian Christians, for in their society slaves were considered to be only pieces of property; women were
kept confined and disrespected; and Gentiles were
constantly sneered at by the Jews.

The Pharisee would pray each morning, "I thank
Thee, God, that I am a Jew, not a Gentile; a man,
not a woman; and a freeman, and not a slave." Yet
all these distinctions are removed "in Christ."

This does not mean that our race, political status,
or sex is changed at conversion; but it does mean
that these things are of no value or handicap when
it comes to our spiritual relationship to God
through Christ. The law perpetuated these distinctions, but God in His grace has declared *all men*
to be on the same level that He might have mercy
upon *all men* (Rom. 11:25-32).

Finally, the law could never make us heirs of
God (Gal. 3:29). God made the promise to "Abraham's seed" (singular, 3:16), and that seed is
Christ. If we are "in Christ" by faith, then we, too,
are "Abraham's seed" spiritually speaking. This

means we are heirs of the spiritual blessings God promised to Abraham. This does not mean that the material and national blessings promised to Israel are set aside, but that Christians today are enriched spiritually because of God's promise to Abraham (see Rom. 11:13 ff.).

This section of Galatians is valuable to us as we read the Old Testament Scriptures. It shows us that the spiritual lessons of the Old Testament are not for the Jews only but have application to Christians today (see Rom. 15:4 and 1 Cor. 10:11-12). In the Old Testament we have *preparation for Christ;* in the Gospels, the *presentation of Christ;* and in the Acts through Revelation, the *appropriation of Christ.*

Your Christian life ought to take on new wonder and meaning as you realize all that you have in Christ. And all of this is by grace—not by law! You are an adult son in God's family, an heir of God. Are you drawing upon your inheritance? This will be Paul's theme in the next section.

Now I say that the heir, as long as he is a child, differeth nothing from a servant, though he be lord of all; but is under tutors and governors until the time appointed of the father. Even so we, when we were children, were in bondage under the elements of the world.

But when the fulness of the time was come, God sent forth his Son, made of a woman, made under the law, to redeem them that were under the law, that we might receive the adoption of sons.

And because ye are sons, God hath sent forth the Spirit of His Son into your hearts, crying, "Abba, Father." Wherefore thou art no more a servant, but a son; and if a son, then an heir of God through Christ.

Howbeit then, when ye knew not God, ye did service unto them which by nature are no gods. But now, after that ye have known God, or rather are known of God, how turn ye again to the weak and beggarly elements, whereunto ye desire again to be in bondage? Ye observe days, and months, and times, and years. I am afraid of you, lest I have bestowed upon you labor in vain.

Brethren, I beseech you, be as I am; for I am as ye are: ye have not injured me at all. Ye know how through infirmity of the flesh I preached the Gospel unto you at the first. And my temptation which was in my flesh ye despised not, nor rejected; but received me as an angel of God, even as Christ Jesus.

Where is then the blessedness ye spake of? For I bear you record, that, if it had been possible, ye would have plucked out your own eyes, and have given them to me. Am I therefore become your enemy, because I tell you the truth?

They zealously affect you, but not well; yea, they would exclude you, that ye might affect them. But it is good to be zealously affected always in a good thing, and not only when I am present with you.

7

It's Time
to Grow Up!

One of the tragedies of legalism is that it gives the appearance of spiritual maturity when, in reality, it leads the believer back into a "second childhood" of Christian experience. The Galatian Christians, like most believers, wanted to grow and go forward for Christ; but they were going about it in the wrong way. Their experience is not too different from that of Christians today who get involved in various legalistic movements, hoping to become better Christians. Their motives may be right, but their methods are wrong.

This is the truth Paul is trying to get across to his beloved converts in Galatia. The Judaizers had bewitched them into thinking that the law would make them better Christians. Their old nature felt an attraction for the law because the law enabled them to *do* things and measure external results. As they measured themselves and their achievements, they felt a sense of accomplishment, and, no doubt, a little bit of pride. They thought they were going forward when actually they were regressing.

Such people are in a situation similar to the airplane passengers who heard their pilot announce: "Our navigator has lost our position, folks, and we have been flying rather aimlessly for over an hour. That's the bad news. But the good news is that we are making very good time."

Paul takes three approaches in this section as he seeks to convince the Galatians that they do not need legalism in order to live the Christian life. They have all they need in Jesus Christ.

1. He Explains Their Adoption (4:1-7)

Among the blessings of the Christian experience is *adoption* (Gal. 4:5; Eph. 1:5). We do not *enter* God's family by adoption, the way a homeless child would enter a loving family in our own society. The only way to get into God's family is by *regeneration,* being "born again" (John 3:3).

The New Testament word for *adoption* means "to place as an adult son." It has to do with our *standing* in the family of God: we are not little children but adult sons with all of the privileges of sonship.

It is unfortunate that many translations of the New Testament do not make a distinction between *children of God* and *sons of God.* We are the children of God by faith in Christ, born into God's family. But every child of God is automatically placed into the family as a *son,* and as a son he has all the legal rights and privileges of a son. When a sinner trusts Christ and is saved, as far as his *condition* is concerned, he is a "spiritual babe" who needs to grow (1 Peter 2:2-3); but as far as his *position* is concerned, he is an adult son who can draw upon the Father's wealth and who can exercise all the wonderful privileges of sonship.

We *enter* God's family by regeneration, but we

enjoy God's family by adoption. The Christian does not have to wait to begin enjoying the spiritual riches he has in Christ. "If a son, then an heir of God through Christ" (Gal. 4:7). Now follows Paul's discussion about adoption. He reminds his readers of three facts.

What we were: children in bondage (4:1-3). No matter how wealthy a father may be, his infant son or toddling child cannot really enjoy that wealth. In the Roman world, the children of wealthy people were cared for by slaves. No matter who his father was, the child was still a child, under the supervision of a servant. In fact, the child himself was not much different from the servant who guarded him. The servant was commanded by the master of the house, and the child was commanded by the servant.

This was the spiritual condition of the Jews under the age of the law. The law, you recall, was the "guardian" that disciplined the nation and prepared the people for the coming of Christ (Gal. 3:23-25). So, when the Judaizers led the Galatians back into legalism, they were leading them not only into religious bondage, but also into moral and spiritual infancy and immaturity.

Paul states that the Jews were, like little children, in bondage to "the elements of the world." This word *elements* means *the basic principles, the ABCs*. For some 15 centuries, Israel had been in kindergarten and grade school, learning their "spiritual ABCs," so that they would be ready when Christ would come. Then they would get the full revelation, for Jesus Christ is "the Alpha and the Omega" (Rev. 22:13); He encompasses *all* the alphabet of God's revelation to man. He is God's last Word (Heb. 1:1-3).

Legalism, then, is not a step toward maturity; it is a step back into childhood. The law was not God's final revelation; it was but the preparation for that final revelation in Christ. It is important that a person know his ABCs, because they are the foundation for understanding all of the language. But the man who sits in a library and recites the ABCs instead of reading the great literature that is around him, is showing that he is immature and ignorant, not mature and wise. Under the law, the Jews were children in bondage, not sons enjoying liberty.

What God did: redeemed us (4:4-5). The expression *the fulness of the time* (v. 4) refers to that time when the world was providentially ready for the birth of the Saviour. Historians tell us that the Roman world was in great expectation, waiting for a deliverer, at the time when Jesus was born. The old religions were dying; the old philosophies were empty and powerless to change men's lives. Strange new mystery religions were invading the empire. Religious bankruptcy and spiritual hunger were everywhere. God was preparing the world for the arrival of His Son.

From the historical point of view, the Roman Empire itself helped prepare the world for the birth of the Saviour. Roads connected city with city, and all cities ultimately with Rome. Roman laws protected the rights of citizens, and Roman soldiers guarded the peace. Thanks to both the Greek and Roman conquests, Latin and Greek were known across the Empire. Christ's birth at Bethlehem was not an accident; it was an appointment: Jesus came in "the fulness of the time." (And, it is worth noting, that He will come again when the time is ready.)

Paul is careful to point out the dual nature of

Jesus Christ (v. 4), that He is both God and man. As God, Jesus "came forth" (John 16:28); but as man, He was "made of a woman." The ancient promise said that the Redeemer would be of "the woman's seed" (Gen. 3:15); and Jesus fulfilled that promise (Isa. 7:14; Matt. 1:18-25).

Paul has told us *who* came—God's Son; he has told us *when* He came and *how* He came. Now he explains *why* He came: "to redeem them that were under the law" (Gal. 4:5). *Redeem* is the same word Paul used earlier (3:13); it means "to set free by paying a price." A man could purchase a slave in any Roman city (there were about 60,000,000 slaves in the empire), either to keep the slave for himself or to set him free. Jesus came to set us free. So, to go back into the law is to undo the very work of Christ on the cross. He did not purchase us to make us slaves, but *sons!* Under law, the Jews were mere children, but under grace, the believer is a son of God with an adult standing in God's family.

Perhaps at this point a chart will help us understand better the contrast between being a "child of God" and a "son of God."

the child	*the son*
by regeneration	by adoption
entering the family	enjoying the family
under guardians	the liberty of an adult
cannot inherit	an heir of the Father

What we are: sons and heirs (4:6-7). Once again, the whole Trinity is involved in our spiritual experience: God the Father sent the Son to die for us, and God the Son sent His Spirit to live in us. The contrast here is not between immature children and adult sons, but between *servants* and *sons*. Like the prodigal son, the Galatians wanted their Father to accept them as servants, when they really were sons (Luke 15:18-19). The contrasts are easy to see. For example:

The son has the same nature as the father, but the servant does not. When we trust Christ, the Holy Spirit comes to live within us; and this means we are "partakers of the divine nature" (2 Peter 1:4). The law could never give a person God's nature within. All it could do was reveal to the person his desperate need for God's nature. So, when the believer goes back into law, he is denying the very divine nature within, and he is giving the old nature (the flesh) opportunity to go to work.

The son has a father, while the servant has a master. No servant could ever say "Father" to his master. When the sinner trusts Christ, he receives the Holy Spirit within, and the Spirit tells him that he is a child of the Father (Rom. 8:15-16). It is natural for a baby to cry, but not for a baby to talk to his father. When the Spirit enters the heart, He says, "Abba, Father" (Gal. 4:6); and, in response, the believer cries, "Abba, Father!" (Rom. 8:15). The word *Abba* is an Aramaic word that is the equivalent of our English word "papa." This shows the closeness of the child to the Father. No servant has this.

The son obeys out of love, while the servant obeys out of fear. The Spirit works in the *heart* of the believer to quicken and increase his love for God. "The fruit of the Spirit is love" (Gal. 5:22). "The love of God is shed abroad in our hearts by the Holy [Spirit]" (Rom. 5:5). The Judaizers told the Galatians that they would become better Christians by submitting to the law, but the law can never produce obedience. Only love can do that. "If ye love Me, keep My commandments" (John 14:15).

The son is rich, while the servant is poor. We are both "sons and heirs." And since we are adopted—placed as adult sons in the family—we may begin drawing upon our inheritance right now. God has made available to us the riches of His grace (Eph. 1:7; 2:7), the riches of His glory (Phil. 4:19), the riches of His goodness (Rom. 2:4), and the riches of His wisdom (Rom. 11:33 ff.)—and all of the riches of God are found in Christ (Col. 1:19; 2:3).

The son has a future, while the servant does not. While many kind masters did provide for their slaves in old age, it was not required of them. The father always provides for the son (2 Cor. 12:14).

In one sense, our adoption is not yet final, because we are awaiting the return of Christ and the redemption of our bodies (Rom. 8:23). Some scholars think that this second stage in our adoption corresponds to the Roman practice when a man adopted someone outside his family to be his son. First there was a *private* ceremony at which the son was purchased; then there was a *public* ceremony at which the adoption was declared openly before the officials.

Christians have experienced the first stage: we have been purchased by Christ and indwelt by the Spirit. We are awaiting the second stage: the public declaration at the return of Christ when "we shall be like Him" (1 John 3:1-3). We are "sons and heirs," and the best part of our inheritance is yet to come (see 1 Peter 1:1-5).

2. He Laments Their Regression (4:8-11)

What really happened when the Galatians turned

from grace to law? To begin with, they abandoned
liberty for bondage. When they were ignorant sinners, they had served their false gods and had experienced the tragedy of such pagan slavery. But
then they had trusted Christ and been delivered
from superstition and slavery. Now they were
abandoning their liberty in Christ and going back
into bondage. They were "dropping out" of the
school of grace and enrolling in the kindergarten
of law! They were destroying all the good work the
Lord had done in them through Paul's ministry.

The phrase *weak and beggarly elements* tells us
the extent of their regression. They were giving
up the power of the Gospel for the weakness of
law, and the wealth of the Gospel for the poverty
of law. The law never made anybody rich or pow-
erful; on the contrary, the law could only reveal
man's weakness and spiritual bankruptcy. No
wonder Paul weeps over these believers, as he sees
them abandon liberty for bondage, power for weakness, and wealth for poverty.

How were they doing this? By adopting the Old
Testament system of religion with its special ob-
servations of "days, and months, and times, and
years" (v. 10).

Does this mean that it is wrong for Christians
to set aside one day a year to remember the birth
of Christ? Or that a special observance of the coming of the Spirit at Pentecost, or the blessing of the
harvest in autumn, is a sin?

Not necessarily. If we observe special days like
slaves, hoping to gain some spiritual merit, then
we are sinning. But if in the observance, we express
our liberty in Christ and let the Spirit enrich us
with His grace, then the observance can be a spiritual blessing.

The New Testament makes it clear that Christians are not to legislate religious observances for each other (Rom. 14:4-13). We are not to praise the man who celebrates the day, nor are we to condemn the man who does not celebrate. But if a man thinks he is saving his soul, or automatically growing in grace, because of a religious observance, then he is guilty of legalism.

Our evangelical churches have many different kinds of observances, and it is wrong for us to go beyond the Word of God in comparing, criticizing, or condemning. But all of us must beware of that legalistic spirit that caters to the flesh, leads to pride, and makes the outward event a substitute for the inward experience.

3. He Seeks Their Affection (4:12-18)

Paul was a wonderful spiritual father; he knew just how to balance rebuke with love. Now he turns from "spanking" to "embracing" as he reminds the believers of their love for him and his love for them. At one point they were willing to sacrifice anything for Paul, so great was their love; but now he had become their enemy. The Judaizers had come in and stolen their affection.

Bible students wish Paul had been more explicit here, because we are not sure just what events he is talking about. When Paul had originally visited them, he was suffering from some physical affliction. If, as noted in chapter 1, Paul wrote this letter to the churches of South Galatia, then he is referring to his first missionary journey, recorded in Acts 13—14. Apparently Paul had not intended to visit these cities, but was forced to do so because of some bodily infirmity. We can only speculate as to what this was. Some have suggested malaria;

others, an affliction of the eyes (see Gal. 4:15).
Whatever it was, it must have made Paul somewhat repulsive in appearance, because he com-
mends the Galatians for the way they received him
in spite of the way he looked. To them, he was an
angel of God. It is a wonderful thing when people
accept God's servants, not because of their outward
appearance, but because they represent the Lord
and bring His message.

Now Paul asks them: "What has happened to
that love? What has happened to the blessedness—
the happiness—you experienced when you heard
the Gospel and trusted Christ?" Of course, Paul
knew what had happened: the Judaizers had come
in and stolen their hearts.

One of the marks of a false teacher is that he
tries to attract other men's converts to himself, and
not simply to the truth of the Word or to the Person of Jesus Christ. It was not the Judaizers who
originally came to Galatia and led them to Christ;
it was Paul. Like the cultists today, these false
teachers were not winning lost sinners to Christ,
but were stealing converts from those who were
truly serving the Lord. Paul had proved to be their
loving friend. He had "become as they were" by
identifying himself with them (v. 12). Now they
were turning away from Paul and following false
shepherds.

Paul told them the truth, but the Judaizers told
them lies. Paul sought to glorify Christ, but the
Judaizers glorified themselves and their converts.
"Those people are zealous to win you over, but for
no good. What they want is to alienate you from
us, so that you may be zealous for them" (v. 17,
NIV).

A true servant of God does not "use people" to

build himself up or his work; he ministers in love to help people know Christ better and glorify Him. Beware of that religious worker who wants your exclusive allegiance because he is the only one who is right. He will use you as long as he can and then drop you for somebody else—and your fall will be a painful one. The task of the spiritual leader is to get people to love and follow Christ, not to promote himself and his ministry.

"Faithful are the wounds of a friend, but the kisses of an enemy are deceitful" (Prov. 27:6). Paul had proved his love to the Galatians by telling them the truth; but they would not accept it. They were enjoying the "kisses" of the Judaizers, not realizing that these kisses were leading them into bondage and sorrow. Christ had made them sons and heirs, but they were rapidly becoming slaves and beggars.

They had not lost the *experience* of salvation— they were still Christians, but they were losing the *enjoyment* of their salvation and finding satisfaction in their works instead. Sad to say, *they did not realize their losses.* They actually thought they were becoming better Christians by substituting law for grace, and the religious deeds of the flesh for the fruit of the Spirit.

Is *your* Christian life moving forward into liberty or backward into bondage? Think carefully before you answer.

My little children, of whom I travail in birth again until Christ be formed in you, I desire to be present with you now and to change my voice; for I stand in doubt of you.

Tell me, ye that desire to be under the law, do ye not hear the law? For it is written, that Abraham had two sons, the one by a bondmaid, the other by a freewoman. But he who was of the bondwoman was born after the flesh; but he of the freewoman was by promise.

Which things are an allegory: for these are the two covenants; the one from the mount Sinai, which gendereth to bondage, which is Agar. For this Agar is mount Sinai in Arabia, and answereth to Jerusalem which now is, and is in bondage with her children. But Jerusalem which is above is free, which is the mother of us all.

For it is written, "Rejoice, thou barren that bearest not; break forth and cry, thou that travailest not: for the desolate hath many more children than she which hath an husband."

Now we, brethren, as Isaac was, are the children of promise. But as then he that was born after the flesh persecuted him that was born after the Spirit, even so it is now.

Nevertheless what saith the Scripture? "Cast out the bondwoman and her son: for the son of the bondwoman shall not be heir with the son of the freewoman." So then, brethren, we are not children of the bondwoman, but of the free.

8

Meet Your Mother

We parents never seem to outgrow our children. "When they're little, they're a handful; but when they're grown, they're a heartful!" I remember hearing my mother say, "When they're little, they step on your toes; but when they're grown, they step on your heart."

This is what Paul was experiencing as he tried to help the Galatian believers with their confused spiritual lives. When he had first come to them with the Gospel, he had "travailed" spiritually to see them turn to the Lord. But, after all, the Lord Jesus had travailed on the cross to make possible their salvation (Isa. 53:11), and Paul's travail was nothing in comparison. But now the Galatian Christians were falling back into legalism and a "second childhood" experience; and Paul had to travail over them again. He longed to see Christ formed in them, just as we parents long to see our children mature in the will of God.

Since the Judaizers appealed to the law, Paul accepts their challenge and uses the law to prove that Christians are not under the law. He takes the familiar story of Ishmael and Isaac (Gen. 16—21) and draws from it basic truths about the Christian's relationship to the Law of Moses.

The events described actually happened, but Paul uses them as an allegory, which is a narrative that has a deeper meaning behind it. Perhaps the most famous allegory in the English language is John Bunyan's *A Pilgrim's Progress,* in which Bunyan traces Christian's experiences from the City of Destruction to heaven. In an allegory, persons and actions represent hidden meanings, so that the narrative can be read on two levels: the literal and the symbolic.

Paul's use of Genesis in this section does not give us license to find "hidden meanings" in all the events of the Old Testament. If we take that approach to the Bible, we can make it mean almost anything we please. This is the way many false teachings arise. The Holy Spirit inspired Paul to discern the hidden meaning of the Genesis story. We must always interpret the Old Testament in the light of the New Testament, and where the New Testament gives us permission, we may search for hidden meanings. Otherwise, we must accept the plain statements of Scripture and not try to "spiritualize" everything.

1. The Historical Facts (4:19-23)

Perhaps the easiest way to grasp the historical account is to trace briefly Abraham's experiences as recorded in Genesis 12 through 21. Using his age as our guide, we will trace the events on which Paul is basing his argument for Christian liberty.

75—Abraham is called by God to go to Canaan; and God promises him many descendants (Gen. 12:1-9). Both Abraham and his wife, Sarah, wanted children, but Sarah was barren. God was waiting until both of them were "as good as dead" before He would perform the miracle of sending them a son (Rom. 4:16-25).

85—The promised son has not yet arrived, and Sarah becomes impatient. She suggests that Abraham marry Hagar, her maid, and try to have a son by her. This act was legal in that society, but it was not in the will of God. Abraham followed her suggestion and married Hagar (Gen. 16:1-3).

86—Hagar gets pregnant and Sarah gets jealous! Things are so difficult in the home that Sarah throws Hagar out. But the Lord intervenes, sends Hagar back, and promises to take care of her and her son. When Abraham is 86, the son is born, and he calls him Ishmael (Gen. 16:4-16).

99—God speaks to Abraham and promises again that he will have a son by Sarah and says to call his name Isaac. Later, God appears again and reaffirms the promise to Sarah as well (see Gen. 17—18).

100—The son is born (Gen. 21:1-7). They name him Isaac ("laughter") as commanded by God. But the arrival of Isaac creates a new problem in the home: Ishmael has a rival. For 14 years, Ishmael has been his father's only son, very dear to his heart. How will Ishmael respond to the presence of a rival?

103—It is customary for the Jews to wean their children at about the age of three, and to make a great occasion of it. At the feast, Ishmael starts to mock Isaac (Gen. 21:8 ff.) and to create trouble in the home. There is only one solution to the problem, and a costly one at that: Hagar and her son have to go. With a broken heart, Abraham sends his son away, because this is what the Lord tells him to do (Gen. 21:9-14).

On the surface, this story appears to be nothing more than a tale of a family problem, but beneath the surface are meanings that carry tremendous spiritual power. Abraham, the two wives, and the two sons represent spiritual realities; and their relationships teach us important lessons.

2. The Spiritual Truths (4:24-29)

Paul now explains the meanings that lie behind these historical events; perhaps they are best classified as follows:

The Old Covenant	*The New Covenant*
Law	Grace
Hagar the slave	Sarah the free-woman
Ishmael, conceived after the flesh	Isaac, conceived miraculously
Earthly Jerusalem in bondage	Heavenly Jerusalem, which is free

Paul begins with the two sons, Ishmael and Isaac (4:22-23), and explains that they illustrate our two births: the physical birth that makes us sinners and the spiritual birth that makes us the children of God. As you think about this, and read Genesis 21:1-12, you discover some wonderful spiritual truths about your salvation.

Isaac illustrates the believer in several particulars.

He was born by God's power. In fact, God deliberately waited 25 years before He granted Abraham and Sarah their son. Isaac was "born after the Spirit" (Gal. 4:29), and, of course, the Christian is "born of the Spirit" (John 3:1-7). Isaac came into the world through Abraham (who represents faith,

Gal. 3:9) and Sarah (who represents grace); so that he was born "by grace . . . through faith" as is every true Christian (Eph. 2:8-9).

He brought joy. His name means "laughter," and certainly he brought joy to his aged parents. Salvation is an experience of joy, not only to the believer himself, but also to those around him.

He grew and was weaned (Gen. 21:8). Salvation is the beginning, not the ending. After we are born, we must grow (1 Peter 2:2; 2 Peter 3:18). Along with maturity comes weaning: we must lay aside "childish things" (1 Cor. 13:11). How easy it is for us to hold the "toys" of our earlier Christian days and fail to lay hold of the "tools" of the mature believer. The child does not enjoy being weaned, but he can never become a man until it happens. (Read Ps. 131 at this point.)

He was persecuted (Gen. 21:9). Ishmael (the flesh) caused problems for Isaac, just as our old nature causes problems for us. (Paul will discuss this in detail in Gal. 5:16 ff.) Ishmael created no problems in the home *until Isaac was born,* just as our old nature creates no problems for us until the new nature enters when we yield to Christ. In Abraham's home we see the same basic conflicts that we Christians face today:

Hagar versus Sarah = Law versus Grace

Ishmael versus Isaac = Flesh versus Spirit

It is important to note that *you cannot separate these four factors.* The Judaizers taught that law made the believer more spiritual, but Paul makes it clear that law only releases the opposition of the flesh and a conflict within the believer ensues (see Rom. 7:19). There was no law strong enough either to change or to control Ishmael, *but Isaac never needed any law.* It has well been said, "The old nature knows no law and the new nature needs no law."

Having explained the significance of the two sons, Paul now turns to an explanation of the two wives, Sarah and Hagar. He is illustrating the contrasts between Law and Grace and is proving that the believer is not under law but is under the loving freedom that comes through God's grace. Notice, then, the facts about Hagar that prove that the law no longer has power over the Christian.

Hagar was Abraham's second wife. God did not *begin* with Hagar; he began with Sarah.

As far as God's dealings with men are concerned, *God began with grace.* In Eden, God provided for Adam and Eve by grace. Even after they sinned, in His grace He provided them with coats of skins for a covering (Gen. 3:21). He did not give them laws to obey as a way of redemption; instead, He gave them a gracious promise to believe: the promise of a victorious Redeemer (Gen. 3:15).

In His relationship with Israel also, God first operated on the basis of grace, not law. His covenant with Abraham (Gen. 15) was all of grace, because Abraham was in a deep sleep when the covenant was established. When God delivered Israel from Egypt, it was on the basis of grace and not law, for the law had not yet been given. Like Hagar, Abraham's second wife, the law was "added" (Gal. 3:19). Hagar performed a function temporarily, and then moved off the scene, just as the law performed a special function and then was taken away (3:24-25).

Hagar was a slave. Five times in this section she is called a "bondmaid" or "bondwoman" (vv. 22-23, 30-31). Sarah was a freewoman, and therefore her position was one of liberty; but Hagar, even

though married to Abraham, was still a servant.
Likewise, the law was given *as a servant.* "Wherefore then serveth the Law?" (3:19) It served as a
mirror to reveal men's sins (Rom. 3:20) and as a
monitor to control men and ultimately lead them
to Christ (Gal. 3:23-25); but the law was never
meant to be *a mother!*

Hagar was not meant to bear a child. Abraham's
marriage to Hagar was out of the will of God; it
was the result of Sarah's and Abraham's unbelief
and impatience. Hagar was trying to do what only
Sarah could do, and it failed. The law cannot give
life (Gal. 3:21), or righteousness (2:21), or the
gift of the Spirit (3:2), or a spiritual inheritance
(3:18). Isaac was born Abraham's heir (Gen. 21:
10), but Ishmael could not share in this inheritance. The Judaizers were trying to make Hagar a
mother again, while Paul was in spiritual travail for
his converts that they might become more like
Christ. No amount of religion or legislation can give
the dead sinner life. Only Christ can do that through
the Gospel.

Hagar gave birth to a slave. Ishmael was "a
wild man" (Gen. 16:12), and even though he was
a slave, nobody could control him, including his
mother. Like Ishmael, the old nature (the flesh)
is at war with God, and the law cannot change or
control it. By nature, the Spirit and the flesh are
"contrary the one to the other" (Gal. 5:17), and
no amount of religious activity is going to change
the picture. Whoever chooses Hagar (Law) for his
mother is going to experience bondage (4:8-11, 22-
25, 30-31; 5:1). But whoever chooses Sarah (Grace)
for his mother is going to enjoy liberty in Christ.
God wants His children to be free (5:1).

Hagar was cast out. It was Sarah who gave the

order: "Cast out this bondwoman and her son"
(Gen. 21:9-10), and God subsequently approved it
(Gen. 21:12). Ishmael had been in the home for at
least 17 years, but his stay was not to be permanent;
eventually he had to be cast out. There was not
room in the household for Hagar and Ishmael with
Sarah and Isaac; one pair had to go.

It is impossible for law and grace, the flesh and
the Spirit, to compromise and stay together. God
did not ask Hagar and Ishmael to make occasional
visits to the home; the break was permanent. The
Judaizers in Paul's day—and in our own day—are
trying to reconcile Sarah and Hagar, and Isaac and
Ishmael; such reconciliation is contrary to the Word
of God. It is impossible to mix law and grace, faith
and works, God's gift of righteousness and man's
attempts to earn righteousness.

Hagar was not married again. God never gave
the law any other nation or people, including His
Church. For the Judaizers to impose the law upon
the Galatian Christians was to oppose the very plan
of God. In Paul's day, the nation of Israel was under
bondage to the law, while the Church was enjoying
liberty under the gracious rule of the "Jerusalem
which is above" (Gal. 4:26). The Judaizers wanted
to "wed" Mt. Sinai and the heavenly Mt. Zion (Heb.
12:22), but to do this would be to deny what Jesus
did on Mt. Calvary (Gal. 2:21). Hagar is not to be
married again.

From the human point of view, it might seem
cruel that God should command Abraham to send
away his own son Ishmael, whom he loved very
much. But it was the only solution to the problem,
for "the wild man" could never live with the child
of promise. In a deeper sense, however, think of
what it cost God when He gave His Son to bear

the curse of the law to set us free. Abraham's broken heart meant Isaac's liberty; God's giving of His Son means our liberty in Christ.

3. The Practical Blessings (4:30-31)

We Christians, like Isaac, are the children of promise by grace. The covenant of grace, pictured by Sarah, is our spiritual mother. The law and the old nature (Hagar and Ishmael) want to persecute us and bring us into bondage. How are we to solve this problem?

We can try to change them. This must fail, for we cannot change either the law or the old nature. "That which is born of the flesh is flesh" (John 3:6), and, we might add, *it always will be flesh.* God did not try to change Ishmael and Hagar, either by force or by education; neither can you and I change the old nature and the law.

We can try to compromise with them. This did not work in Abraham's home, and neither will it work in our lives. The Galatians were trying to effect such a compromise, but it was only leading them gradually into bondage. False teachers today tell us, "Don't abandon Christ; simply move into a deeper Christian life by practicing the law along with your faith in Christ." Invite Hagar and Ishmael back home again. But this is a path back into slavery: "How turn ye again to the weak and beggarly elements, whereunto ye desire again to be in bondage?" (Gal. 4:9)

We can cast them out. This is what we are supposed to do. First, Paul applies this to the nation of Israel (vv. 25-27); then he applies it to the individual Christian. The nation of Israel had been in bondage under the law, but this was a temporary thing, preparing them for the coming of Christ. Now that Christ had come, law had to go. Jesus Christ, like Isaac, was a child of promise, born by the miraculous power of God. Once He had come and died for the people, the law had to go.

Paul quotes Isaiah (54:1), applying his words to Sarah who was barren before the birth of Isaac; but also applying it to the Church (Gal. 4:27). Note the contrasts:

Israel	*The Church*
earthly Jerusalem	heavenly Jerusalem
bondage	freedom
barren legalism	fruitful grace

Sarah had been barren, and she tried to become fruitful by having Abraham marry Hagar. This failed and brought only trouble. *The law cannot give life or fruitfulness; legalism is barren.* For the Early Church to go back into bondage would mean barrenness and disobedience to the Word of God. Because it held fast to grace, it spread across the world in fruitfulness.

But individual churches and Christians can make the same mistake the Galatians were making: they can fail to cast out Hagar and Ishmael. *Legalism* is one of the major problems among Christians today. We must keep in mind that *legalism* does not mean the setting of spiritual standards; it means worshiping these standards and thinking that we are spiritual because we obey them. It also means judging other believers on the basis of these standards. A person can refrain from smoking, drinking, and attending theaters, for example, *and still not be spiritual.* The Pharisees had high standards; yet they crucified Jesus.

The old nature loves legalism, because it gives

the old nature a chance to "look good." It costs very little for Ishmael not to do certain bad things, or to do certain religious deeds, just so long as he can remain Ishmael. For 17 years Ishmael caused no trouble in the home; and then Isaac came along, and there was conflict. Legalism caters to Ishmael. The Christian who claims to be spiritual because of what he doesn't do is only fooling himself. It takes more than negations to make a positive, fruitful spiritual life.

No doubt the Judaizers were attractive people. They carried credentials from religious authorities (2 Cor. 3:1). They had high standards and were careful in what they ate and drank. They were effective in making converts and liked to advertise their accomplishments (Gal. 6:12-14; 4:17-18). They had rules and standards to cover every area of life, making it easy for their followers to know who was "spiritual" and who was not. But the Judaizers were leading the people into bondage and defeat, not liberty and victory, *and the people did not know the difference.*

In the closing chapters of this letter, Paul will point out the greatest tragedy of legalism: it gives opportunity for the flesh to work. The old nature cannot be controlled by law; eventually it has to break out—and when it does, watch out! This explains why legalistic religious groups often have fights and divisions ("ye fight and devour one another," Gal. 5:15), and often are plagued with the defiling sins of the flesh (5:19 ff.). While every church has its share of these problems, it is especially prominent in those groups where there is an atmosphere of legalism. When you invite Hagar and Ishmael to live with Sarah and Isaac, you are inviting trouble.

Thank God, the Christian is set free from the curse of the law and the control of the law. "Cast out the bondwoman and her son." It may pain us deeply, as it did Abraham; but it must be done. To attempt to mix law and grace is to attempt the impossible. It makes for a frustrated, barren Christian life. But to live by grace, through faith, gives one a free and fulfilling Christian life.

What is the secret? The Holy Spirit. And it is this secret that Paul will share in the closing "practical" chapters of the letter. Meanwhile, you and I need to beware lest Ishmael and Hagar have crept back into our lives. If they have—let us cast them out.

Part III
Practical Section:

Grace and
the Christian Life

Chapters 5—6

Stand fast therefore in the liberty wherewith Christ hath made us free, and be not entangled again with the yoke of bondage.

Behold, I Paul say unto you, that if ye be circumcised, Christ shall profit you nothing. For I testify again to every man that is circumcised, that he is a debtor to do the whole law. Christ is become of no effect unto you, whosoever of you are justified by the law; ye are fallen from grace.

For we through the Spirit wait for the hope of righteousness by faith. For in Jesus Christ neither circumcision availeth any thing, nor uncircumcision; but faith which worketh by love.

Ye did run well; who did hinder you that ye shculd not obey the truth? This persuasion cometh not of Him that calleth you. A little leaven leaventh the whole lump.

I have confidence in you through the Lord, that ye will be none otherwise minded: but he that troubleth you shall bear his judgment, whosoever he be.

And I, brethren, if I yet preach circumcision, why do I yet suffer persecution? Then is the offense of the cross ceased. I would they were even cut off which trouble you.

9

Stop!
Thief!

"Paul's doctrine of grace is dangerous!" cried the Judaizers. "It replaces law with license. Why, if we do away with our rules and abandon our high standards, the churches will fall apart."

First-century Judaizers are not the only ones afraid to depend on God's grace. Legalists in our churches today warn that we dare not teach people about the liberty we have in Christ lest it result in religious anarchy. These people misunderstand Paul's teaching about grace, and it is to correct such misunderstanding that Paul wrote the final section of his letter (Gal. 5—6).

Paul turns now from argument to application, from the doctrinal to the practical. The Christian who lives by faith is not going to become a rebel. Quite the contrary, he is going to experience the *inner discipline* of God that is far better than the outer discipline of man-made rules. No man could become a rebel who depends on God's grace, yields to God's Spirit, lives for others, and seeks to glorify God. The *legalist* is the one who eventually rebels, because he is living in bondage, depending on the flesh, living for self, and seeking the praise of men and not the glory of God.

No, Paul's doctrine of Christian liberty through grace is not the dangerous doctrine. It is *legalism* that is the dangerous doctrine, because legalism attempts to do the impossible: change the old nature and make it obey the laws of God. Legalism succeeds for a short time, and then the flesh begins to rebel. The surrendered Christian who depends on the power of the Spirit is not *denying* the law of God, or rebelling against it. Rather, that law is *being fulfilled in him* through the Spirit (Rom. 8:1-4). It is easy to see the sequence of thought in these closing chapters:

1. I have been set free by Christ. I am no longer under bondage to the law (Gal. 5:1-12).

2. But I need something—Someone—to control my life from within. That Someone is the Holy Spirit (5:13-26).

3. Through the Spirit's love, I have a desire to live for others, not for self (6:1-10).

4. This life of liberty is so wonderful, I want to live it to the glory of God; for He is the One making it possible (6:11-18).

Now, contrast this with the experience of the person who chooses to live under law, under the discipline of some religious leader.

1. If I obey these rules, I will become a more spiritual person. I am a great admirer of this religious leader, so I now submit myself to his system.

2. I believe I have the strength to obey and improve myself. I do what I am told, and measure up to the standards set for me.

3. I'm making progress. I don't do some of the things I used to do. Other people compliment me on my obedience and discipline. I can see that I

am better than others in my fellowship. How wonderful to be so spiritual.

4. If only others were like me! God is certainly fortunate that I am His. I have a desire to share this with others so they can be as I am. Our group is growing and we have a fine reputation. Too bad other groups are not as spiritual as we are.

No matter how you look at it, legalism is an insidious, dangerous enemy. *When you abandon grace for law, you always lose.* In this first section (5:1-12), Paul explains what the believer loses when he turns from God's grace to man-made rules and regulations.

1. The Slave—You Lose Your Liberty (5:1)

Paul has used two comparisons to show his readers what the Law is really like: a schoolmaster or guardian (3:24; 4:2), a bondwoman (4:22 ff.); now he compares it to a yoke of slavery. You will recall that Peter used this same image at the famous conference in Jerusalem (see Acts 15:10).

The image of the yoke is not difficult to understand. It usually represents slavery, service, and control by someone else over your life; it may also represent willing service and submission to someone else. When God delivered Israel from Egyptian servitude, it was the breaking of a yoke (Lev. 26:13). The farmer uses the yoke to control and guide his oxen, because they would not willingly serve if they were free.

When the believers in Galatia trusted Christ, they lost the yoke of servitude to sin and put on the yoke of Christ (Matt. 11:28-30). The yoke of religion is hard, and the burdens heavy; Christ's yoke is "easy" and His burden is "light." That word *easy* in the Greek means "kind, gracious." The yoke of Christ *frees* us to fulfill His will, while the yoke of the law *enslaves* us. The unsaved person wears a yoke of sin (Lam. 1:14); the religious legalist wears the yoke of bondage (Gal. 5:1); but the Christian who depends on God's grace wears the liberating yoke of Christ.

It is Christ who has made us free from the bondage of the law. He freed us from the curse of the law by dying for us on the tree (Gal. 3:13). The believer is no longer under law; he is under grace (Rom. 6:14). This does not mean that we are outlaws and rebels. It simply means that we no longer need the *external* force of law to keep us in God's will, because we have the *internal* leading of the Holy Spirit of God (Rom. 8:1-4). Christ died to set us free, not to make us slaves. To go back to law is to become entangled in a maze of "do's and don'ts" and to abandon spiritual adulthood for a "second childhood."

Sad to say, there are some people who feel very insecure with liberty. They would rather be under the tyranny of some leader than to make their own decisions freely. There are some believers who are frightened by the liberty they have in God's grace; so they seek out a fellowship that is legalistic and dictatorial, where they can let others make their decisions for them. This is comparable to an adult climbing back into the crib. The way of Christian liberty is the way of fulfillment in Christ. No wonder Paul issues that ultimatum: "Do not be entangled again in the yoke of bondage. Take your stand for liberty."

2. The Debtor—You Lose Your Wealth (5:2-6)

Paul uses three phrases to describe the losses the Christian incurs when he turns from grace to law:

"Christ shall profit you nothing" (v. 2); "a debtor to do the whole law" (v. 3); "Christ is become of no effect unto you" (v. 4). This leads to the sad conclusion in verse 4: "Ye are fallen from grace." It is bad enough that legalism robs the believer of his liberty, but it also robs him of his spiritual wealth in Christ. The believer living under law becomes a bankrupt slave.

God's Word teaches that when we were unsaved, we owed God a debt we could not pay. Jesus makes this clear in His parable of the two debtors (Luke 7:36-50). Two men owed money to a creditor, the one owing 10 times as much as the other. But neither was able to pay, so the creditor "graciously forgave them both" (literal translation). No matter how much morality a man may have, he still comes short of the glory of God. Even if his sin debt is one-tenth that of others, he stands unable to pay, bankrupt at the judgment bar of God. God in His grace, because of the work of Christ on the cross, is able to forgive sinners, no matter how large their debt may be.

Thus when we trust Christ, *we become spiritually rich*. We now share in the riches of God's grace (Eph. 1:7), the riches of His glory (Eph. 1:18; Phil. 4:19), the riches of His wisdom (Rom. 11:33), and the "unsearchable riches of Christ" (Eph. 3:8). In Christ we have "all the treasures of wisdom and knowledge" (Col. 2:3), and we are "complete in Him" (Col. 2:10). Once a person is "in Christ," he has all that he needs to live the kind of Christian life God wants him to live.

The Judaizers, however, want us to believe that we are "missing something," that we would be more "spiritual" if we practiced the law with its demands and disciplines. But Paul makes it clear that *the*

law adds nothing—because *nothing can be added!*
Instead, the law comes in as a thief and robs the
believer of the spiritual riches he has in Christ. It
puts him back into bankruptcy, responsible for a
debt he is unable to pay.

To live by grace means to depend on God's abun-
dant supply of every need. To live by law means
to depend on my own strength—the flesh—and be
left to get by without God's supply. Paul warns the
Galatians that to submit to circumcision in these
circumstances would rob them of all the benefits
they have in Christ (though circumcision itself is
an indifferent matter—v. 6; 6:15). Furthermore, to
submit would put them under obligation to obey
the whole law.

It is at this point that legalists reveal their hy-
pocrisy, for they fail to keep the *whole* law. They
look upon the Old Testament law the way a cus-
tomer surveys the food in a cafeteria: they choose
what they want and leave the rest. But this is not
honest. To teach that a Christian today should, for
example, keep the Sabbath but not the Passover,
is to dismember God's law. The same Lawgiver who
gave the one commandment also gave the other
(James 2:9-11). Earlier, Paul had quoted Moses to
prove that the curse of the law is upon everyone
who fails to keep *all* the law (Gal. 3:10; see Deut.
27:26).

Imagine a motorist driving down a city street
and either deliberately or unconsciously driving
through a red light. He is pulled over by a policeman who asks to see his driver's license. Immediately the driver begins to defend himself. "Officer,
I know I ran that red light—but I have never
robbed anybody. I've never committed adultery.
I've never cheated on my income tax."

The policeman smiles as he writes out the ticket, because he knows that *no amount of obedience can make up for one act of disobedience*. It is one law, and the same law that protects the obedient man punishes the offender. To boast about keeping part of the law while at the same time breaking another part is to confess that I am worthy of punishment.

Now we can better understand what Paul means by "fallen from grace" (Gal. 5:4). Certainly he is not suggesting that the Galatians had "lost their salvation," because throughout this letter he deals with them *as believers.* At least nine times he calls them *brethren,* and he also uses the pronoun *we* (4:28, 31). This Paul would never do if his readers were lost. He boldly states, "And because ye are sons, God hath sent forth the Spirit of His Son into your hearts, crying, 'Abba, Father'" (4:6). If his readers were unsaved, Paul could never write those words.

No, to be "fallen from grace" does not mean to lose salvation. Rather, it means "fallen out of the sphere of God's grace." You cannot mix grace and law. If you decide to live in the sphere of law, then you cannot live in the sphere of grace. The believers in Galatia had been *bewitched* by the false teachers (Gal. 3:1) and thus were *disobeying* the truth. They had *removed* toward another gospel (1:6-9), and had *turned back* to the elementary things of the old religion (4:9). As a result, they had become *entangled* with the yoke of bondage, and this led to their present position: "fallen from grace." And the tragedy of this fall is that they had robbed themselves of all the good things Jesus Christ could do for them.

Paul next presents the life of the believer in the sphere of grace (5:5-6). This enables us to contrast the two ways of life. When you live by grace, you depend on the power of the Spirit; but under law, you must depend on yourself and your own efforts. Faith is not dead; faith *works* (see James 2:14-26). But the efforts of the flesh can never accomplish what faith can accomplish through the Spirit. And faith works *through love*—love for God and love for others. Unfortunately, flesh does not manufacture love; too often it produces selfishness and rivalry (see Gal. 5:15). No wonder Paul pictures the life of legalism as a fall!

When the believer walks by faith, depending on the Spirit of God, he lives in the sphere of God's grace; and all his needs are provided. He experiences the riches of God's grace. And, he always has something to look forward to (5:5): one day Jesus shall return to make us like Himself in perfect righteousness. The law gives no promise for perfect righteousness in the future. The law prepared the way for the first coming of Christ (3:23—4:7), but it cannot prepare the way for the second coming of Christ.

So, the believer who chooses legalism robs himself of spiritual liberty and spiritual wealth. He deliberately puts himself into bondage and bankruptcy.

3. The Runner—You Lose Your Direction (5:7-12)

Paul was fond of athletic illustrations and used them often in his letters. His readers were familiar with the Olympic games as well as other Greek athletic contests that always included foot races. It is important to note that Paul never uses the image of the race to tell people how to be saved. He is always talking to Christians about how to live the Christian life. *A contestant in the Greek games had to be a citizen before he could compete.* We become citizens of heaven through faith in Christ; then the Lord puts us on our course and we run to win the prize (see Phil. 3:12-21). We do not run to be saved; we run because we are already saved and want to fulfill God's will in our lives (Acts 20:24).

"You did run well." When Paul first came to them, they received him "as an angel of God" (Gal. 4: 14). They accepted the Word, trusted the Lord Jesus Christ, and received the Holy Spirit. They had a deep joy that was evident to all, and were willing to make any sacrifice to accommodate Paul (4:15). But now, Paul was their enemy. What had happened?

A literal translation of verse 7 gives us the answer: "You were running well. Who cut in on you so that you stopped obeying the truth?" In the races, each runner was to stay in his assigned lane, but some runners would cut in on their competitors to try to get them off course. This is what the Judaizers had done to the Galatian believers: they cut in on them and forced them to change direction and go on a "spiritual detour." It was not God who did this, because He had called them to run faithfully in the lane marked "Grace."

His explanation changes the figure of speech from athletics to cooking, for Paul introduces the idea of yeast (leaven). In the Old Testament, leaven is generally pictured as a symbol of evil. During Passover, for example, no yeast was allowed in the house (Ex. 12:15-19; 13:7). Worshipers were not permitted to mingle leaven with sacrifices (Ex. 34:25), though there were some exceptions to this rule. Jesus used leaven as a picture of sin when He warned against the "leaven of the

Pharisees" (Matt. 16:6-12); and Paul used leaven as a symbol of sin in the church at Corinth (1 Cor. 5).

Yeast is really a good illustration of sin: it is small, but if left alone it grows and permeates the whole. The false doctrine of the Judaizers was introduced to the Galatian churches in a small way, but, before long, the "yeast" grew and eventually took over.

The spirit of legalism does not suddenly overpower a church. Like leaven, it is introduced secretly, it grows, and before long poisons the whole assembly. In most cases, the *motives* that encourage legalism are good ("We want to have a more spiritual church"), but the *methods* are not scriptural.

It is not wrong to have standards in a church, but we should never think that the standards will make anybody spiritual, or that the keeping of the standards is an evidence of spirituality. How easy it is for the yeast to grow. Before long, we become proud of our spirituality ("puffed up" is the way Paul puts it, 1 Cor. 5:2, and that is exactly what yeast does: it puffs up), and then critical of everybody else's lack of spirituality. This, of course, only feeds the flesh and grieves the Spirit, but we go on our way thinking we are glorifying God.

Every Christian has the responsibility to watch for the *beginnings* of legalism, that first bit of yeast that infects the fellowship and eventually grows into a serious problem. No wonder Paul is so vehement as he denounces the false teachers: "I am suffering persecution because I preach the cross, but these false teachers are popular celebrities because they preach a religion that pampers the flesh and feeds the ego. Do they want to circumcise you? I wish that they themselves were *cut off!*" (Gal. 5:11-12, literal translation)

Since the death and resurrection of Christ, there is no spiritual value to circumcision; it is only a physical operation. Paul wished that the false teachers would *operate on themselves*—"castrate themselves"—so that they could not produce any more "children of slavery."

The believer who lives in the sphere of God's grace is free, rich, and running in the lane that leads to reward and fulfillment. The believer who abandons grace for law is a slave, a pauper, and a runner on a detour. In short, he is a loser. And the only way to become a winner is to "purge out the leaven," the false doctrine that mixes law and grace, and yield to the Spirit of God.

God's grace is sufficient for every demand of life. We are saved by grace (Eph. 2:8-10), and we serve by grace (1 Cor. 15:9-10). Grace enables us to endure suffering (2 Cor. 12:9). It is grace that strengthens us (2 Tim. 2:1), so that we can be victorious soldiers. Our God is the God of *all* grace (1 Peter 5:10). We can come to the throne of grace and find grace to help in every need (Heb. 4:16). As we read the Bible, which is "the word of His grace" (Acts 20:32), the Spirit of Grace (Heb. 10:29) reveals to us how rich we are in Christ.

"And of His fulness have all we received, and grace for grace" (John 1:16).

How rich we are!

For, brethren, ye have been called unto liberty; only use not liberty for an occasion to the flesh, but by love serve one another. For all the law is fulfilled in one word, even in this: "Thou shalt love thy neighbour as thyself." But if ye bite and devour one another, take heed that ye be not consumed one of another.

This I say then, walk in the Spirit, and ye shall not fulfill the lust of the flesh. For the flesh lusteth against the Spirit, and the Spirit against the flesh: and these are contrary the one to the other: so that ye cannot do the things that ye would. But if ye be led of the Spirit, ye are not under the law.

Now the works of the flesh are manifest, which are these: adultery, fornication, uncleanness, lasciviousness, idolatry, witchcraft, hatred, variance, emulations, wrath, strife, seditions, heresies, envyings, murders, drunkenness, revelings, and such like: of the which I tell you before, as I have also told you in time past, that they which do such things shall not inherit the kingdom of God.

But the fruit of the Spirit is love, joy, peace, longsuffering, gentleness, goodness, faith, meekness, temperance: against such there is no law.

And they that are Christ's have crucified the flesh with the affections and lusts.

If we live in the Spirit, let us also walk in the Spirit. Let us not be desirous of vainglory, provoking one another, envying one another.

10

The Fifth Freedom

At the close of an important speech to Congress on January 6, 1941, President Franklin D. Roosevelt shared his vision of the kind of world he wanted to see after the war was over. He envisioned four basic freedoms enjoyed by all people: freedom of speech, freedom of worship, freedom from want, and freedom from fear. To some degree, these freedoms have been achieved on a wider scale than in 1941, but our world still needs another freedom, a fifth freedom. Man needs to be free from himself and the tyranny of his sinful nature.

The legalists thought they had the answer to the problem in laws and threats, but Paul has explained that no amount of legislation can change man's basic sinful nature. It is not law on the *outside*, but love on the *inside* that makes the difference. We need another power within, and that power comes from the Holy Spirit of God.

There are at least 14 references to the Holy Spirit in Galatians. When we believe on Christ, the Spirit comes to dwell within us (3:2). We are "born after the Spirit" as was Isaac (4:29). It is the Holy

Spirit in the heart who gives assurance of salvation (4:6); and it is the Holy Spirit who enables us to live for Christ and glorify Him. The Holy Spirit is not simply a "divine influence"; He is a divine Person, just as are the Father and the Son. What God the Father *planned* for you, and God the Son *purchased* for you on the cross, God the Spirit *personalizes* for you and applies to your life as you yield to Him.

This paragraph is perhaps the most crucial in the entire closing section of Galatians; for in it Paul explains three ministries of the Holy Spirit that enable the believer to enjoy liberty in Christ.

1. The Spirit Enables Us to Fulfill the Law of Love (5:13-15)

We are prone to go to extremes. One believer interprets *liberty* as *license* and thinks he can do whatever he wants to do. Another believer, seeing this error, goes to an opposite extreme and imposes law on everybody. Somewhere between *license* on the one hand and *legalism* on the other hand is true Christian liberty.

So, Paul begins by explaining *our calling:* we are called to liberty. The Christian is a free man. He is free from the *guilt* of sin because he has experienced God's forgiveness. He is free from the *penalty* of sin because Christ died for him on the cross. And he is, through the Spirit, free from the *power* of sin in his daily life. He is also free from the *law* with its demands and threats. Christ bore the curse of the law and ended its tyranny once and for all. We are "called unto liberty" because we are "called into the grace of Christ" (Gal. 1:6). *Grace* and *liberty* go together.

Having explained our calling, Paul then issues

a caution: "Don't allow your liberty to degenerate into license!"

This, of course, is the fear of all people who do not understand the true meaning of the grace of God. "If you do away with rules and regulations," they say, "you will create chaos and anarchy."

Of course, that danger is real, not because God's grace fails, but because men fail of the grace of God (Heb. 12:15). If there is a "true grace of God" (1 Peter 5:12), then there is also a *false* grace of God; and there are false teachers who "change the grace of our God into a license for immorality" (Jude 4, NIV). So, Paul's caution is a valid one. Christian liberty is not a license to sin but an opportunity to serve.

This leads to *a commandment:* "By love serve one another" (Gal. 5:13). The key word, of course, is *love.* The formula looks something like this:

liberty + love = service to others

liberty − love = license (slavery to sin)

"I have an extra day off this week," Carl told his wife as he walked into the kitchen. "I think I'll use it to fix Donna's bike and then take Larry on that musuem trip he's been talking about."

"Fixing a bike and visiting a museum hardly sound like exciting ways to spend a day off," his wife replied.

"It's exciting *if you love your kids!*"

The amazing thing about love is that it takes the place of all the laws God ever gave. "Thou shalt love thy neighbor as thyself" solves every problem in human relations (see Rom. 13:8-14). If you love people (because you love Christ), you will not steal from them, lie about them, envy them, or try in any way to hurt them. Love in the heart is God's substitute for laws and threats.

When our children were small, we lived next to a busy highway, and the children knew they would be spanked if they went near the road. As they grew older, they discovered that obedience brought rewards. They learned to obey not only to escape pain but to gain pleasure. Today we live in a busy, dangerous city, and some of our children drive. But we neither threaten nor bribe them in order to keep them safe. They have a built-in discipline of love that regulates their lives, and they would not deliberately hurt themselves, their parents, or other people. Love has replaced law.

On a much higher level, the Holy Spirit within gives us the love that we need (Rom. 5:5; Gal. 5:6, 22). Apparently the Galatian believers were lacking in this kind of love because they were "biting and devouring one another" and were in danger of destroying one another (Gal. 5:15). The picture here is of wild animals attacking each other. This in itself is proof that law cannot force people to get along with each other. No matter how many rules or standards a church may adopt, they are no guarantee of spirituality. Unless the Holy Spirit of God is permitted to fill hearts with His love, selfishness and competition will reign. Both extremes in the Galatian churches—the legalists and the libertines—were actually destroying the fellowship.

The Holy Spirit does not work in a vacuum. He uses the Word of God, prayer, worship, and the fellowship of believers to build us up in Christ. The believer who spends time daily in the Word and prayer, and who yields to the Spirit's working, is going to enjoy liberty and will help build up the church. Read 2 Corinthians 3 for Paul's explanation of the difference between a spiritual ministry of grace and a carnal ministry of law.

2. The Spirit Enables Us to Overcome the Flesh (5:16-21, 24)

The conflict (5:16-17). Just as Isaac and Ishmael were unable to get along, so the Spirit and the flesh (the old nature) are at war with each other. By "the flesh," of course, Paul does not mean "the body." The human body is not sinful; it is neutral. If the Holy Spirit controls the body, then we walk in the Spirit; but if the flesh controls the body, then we walk in the lusts (desires) of the flesh. The Spirit and the flesh have different appetites, and this is what creates the conflict.

These opposite appetites are illustrated in the Bible in different ways. For example, the sheep is a clean animal and avoids garbage, while the pig is an unclean animal and enjoys wallowing in filth (2 Peter 2:19-22). After the rain ceased and the ark settled, Noah released a raven which never came back (Gen. 8:6-7). The raven is a carrion-eating bird and found plenty to feed on. But when Noah released the dove (a clean bird), it came back (Gen. 8:8-12). The last time he released the dove and it did not return, he knew that it had found a clean place to settle down; therefore the waters had receded.

Our old nature is like the pig and the raven, always looking for something unclean on which to feed. Our new nature is like the sheep and the dove, yearning for that which is clean and holy. No wonder a struggle goes on within the life of the believer! The unsaved man knows nothing of this battle because he does not have the Holy Spirit (Rom. 8:9). Ishmael did not create any problems until Isaac came on the scene.

Note that the Christian cannot simply *will* to overcome the flesh: "These two are opposed to each

other, so that you cannot do anything you please"
(Gal. 5:17, WMS). It is this very problem that Paul
discusses in Romans: "I do not know what I am
doing. For what I want to do I do not do, but what
I hate I do. . . . For what I do is not the good I
want to do; no, the evil I do not want to do—this
I keep on doing" (Rom. 7:15, 19, NIV). Paul is not
denying that there is victory. He is simply pointing
out that we cannot win this victory in our own
strength and by our own will.

The conquest (5:18). The solution is not to pit
our will against the flesh, but to surrender our will
to the Holy Spirit. This verse literally means, "But
if you are *willingly led* by the Spirit, then you are
not under the law." The Holy Spirit writes God's law
on our hearts (Heb. 10:14-17; see 2 Cor. 3) so that
we *desire* to obey Him in love. "I delight to do
Thy will, O my God: yea, Thy law is within my
heart" (Ps. 40:8). Being "led of the Spirit" and
"walking in the Spirit" are the opposites of yielding
to the desires of the flesh.

The crucifixion (5:19-21, 24). Paul now lists
some of the ugly "works of the flesh." (You will find
similar lists in Mark 7:20-23; Rom. 1:29-32; 1 Tim.
1:9-10; 2 Tim. 3:2-5.) The flesh is able to manufacture sin but it can never produce the righteousness of God. "The heart is deceitful above all
things, and desperately wicked" (Jer. 17:9). This
list in Galatians can be divided into three major
categories:

(1) *The sensual sins* (5:19, 21b)

Adultery is illicit sex between married people,
while *fornication* generally refers to the same sin
among unmarried people. *Uncleanness* means just
that: a filthiness of heart and mind that makes the
person defiled. The unclean person sees dirt in

everything (see Titus 1:15). *Lasciviousness* is close to our word debauchery. It speaks of a wanton appetite that knows no shame. It goes without saying that all of these sins were rampant in the Roman Empire. *Drunkenness* and *revellings* (orgies) need no explanation.

(2) *The superstitious sins* (5:20a)

Idolatry, like the sins named above, is with us today. Idolatry is simply putting things ahead of God and people. We are to worship God, love people, and use things, but too often we use people, love self, and worship things, leaving God out of the picture completely. Jesus tells us that whatever we worship, we serve (Matt. 4:10). The Christian who devotes more of himself to his car, house, or boat than he does to serving Christ may be in danger of idolatry (Col. 3:5).

The word *witchcraft* is from the Greek word *pharmakeia,* which means "the use of drugs." Our English word *pharmacy* is derived from this word. Magicians in Paul's day often used drugs to bring about their evil effects. Of course, sorcery is forbidden in the Bible as are all activities of the occult (Deut. 18:9-22).

(3) *The social sins* (5:20b-21a)

Hatred means "enmity," the attitude of mind that defies and challenges others. This attitude leads to variance, which is strife, the outworking of enmity. *Emulations* means jealousies or rivalries. How tragic when Christians compete with one another and try to make one another look bad in the eyes of others. *Wrath* means outbursts of anger, and *strife* carries with it the idea of "self-seeking, selfish ambition," that creates divisions in the church.

Seditions and *heresies* are kindred terms. The

first suggests division, and the second cliques
caused by a party spirit. *Divisions and factions*
would be a fair translation. These are the result of
church leaders promoting themselves and insisting
that the people follow them, not the Lord. (The
word *heresy* in the Greek means "to make a
choice.") *Envyings* suggests the carrying of grudges,
the deep desire for what another has (see Prov.
14:30). *Murders* and *drunkenness* need no elucida-
tion.

The person who *practices* these sins shall not inherit the kingdom of God. Paul is not talking about
an *act* of sin, but a *habit* of sin. There is a false
assurance of salvation that is not based on the Word
of God. The fact that the believer is not under law,
but under grace, is no excuse for sin (Rom. 6:15).
If anything, it is an encouragement to live in obedience to the Lord.

But how does the believer handle the old nature
when it is capable of producing such horrible sins?
The law cannot *change* or *control* the old nature.
The old nature must be crucified (Gal. 5:24). Paul
explains that the believer is identified with Christ
in His death, burial, and resurrection (Rom. 6).
Christ not only died *for* me, but *I died with Christ.*
Christ died for me to remove the *penalty* of my
sin, but I died with Christ to break its *power.*

Paul has mentioned this already in Galatians
(see 2:19-20), and he will mention it again (6:14).
He does not tell *us* to crucify ourselves, because this
is impossible. (Crucifixion is one death a man cannot inflict on himself.) He tells us that the flesh
has already been crucified. It is our responsibility
to *believe* this and *act upon it.* (Paul calls this "reck-
oning" in Rom. 6; you have the same truth presented in Col. 3:5 ff.)

You and I are not debtors to the flesh, but to the Spirit (Rom. 8:12-14). We must accept what God says about the old nature and not try to make it something that it is not. We must not make "provision for the flesh" (Rom. 13:14) by feeding it the things that it enjoys. In the flesh dwells no good thing (Rom. 7:18), so we should put no confidence in the flesh (Phil. 3:3). The flesh is not subject to God's law (Rom. 8:7) and it cannot please God (Rom. 8:8). Only through the Holy Spirit can we "put to death" the deeds that the flesh would do through our body (Rom. 8:13). The Holy Spirit is not only the Spirit of life (Rom. 8:2; Gal. 5:25), but He is also the Spirit of death: He helps us to reckon ourselves dead to sin.

We have seen two ministries of the Spirit of God: He enables us to fulfill the law, and He enables us to overcome the flesh. He has a third ministry as well.

3. The Spirit Enables Us to Produce Fruit (5:22-23, 25-26)

It is one thing to overcome the flesh and *not do* evil things, but quite something else *to do* good things. The legalist might be able to boast that he is not guilty of adultery or murder (but see Matt. 5:21-32), but can anyone see the beautiful graces of the Spirit in his life? Negative goodness is not enough in a life; there must be positive qualities as well.

The contrast between *works* and *fruit* is important. A machine in a factory *works*, and turns out a product, but it could never manufacture fruit. Fruit must grow out of life, and, in the case of the believer, it is the life of the Spirit (Gal. 5:25). When you think of "works" you think of effort, labor, strain,

and toil; when you think of "fruit" you think of
beauty, quietness, the unfolding of life. The flesh
produces "dead works" (Heb. 9:14), but the Spirit
produces living fruit. And this fruit has in it the seed
for still more fruit (Gen. 1:11). Love begets more
love! Joy helps to produce more joy! Jesus is concerned that we produce "fruit . . . more fruit
. . . much fruit" (John 15:2, 5), because this is the
way we glorify Him. The old nature cannot produce fruit; only the new nature can do that.

The New Testament speaks of several different
kinds of "fruit": people won to Christ (Rom. 1:13),
holy living (Rom. 6:22), gifts brought to God (Rom.
15:26-28), good works (Col. 1:10), and praise
(Heb. 13:15). The "fruit of the Spirit" listed in our
passage has to do with *character* (Gal. 5:22-23).
It is important that we distinguish the *gift* of the
Spirit, which is salvation (Acts 2:38; 11:17), and
the *gifts* of the Spirit, which have to do with service (1 Cor. 12), from the *graces* of the Spirit,
which relate to Christian character. It is unfortunate that an overemphasis on gifts has led some
Christians to neglect the graces of the Spirit. Building Christian character must take precedence over
displaying special abilities.

The characteristics that God wants in our lives
are seen in the ninefold fruit of the Spirit. Paul begins with *love* because all of the other fruit is really
an outgrowth of love. Compare these eight qualities with the characteristics of love given to the
Corinthians (see 1 Cor. 13:4-8). This word for love
is *agape*, which means divine love. (The Greek
word *eros*, meaning "sensual love," is never used
in the New Testament.) This divine love is God's
gift to us (Rom 5:5), and we must cultivate it and
pray that it will increase (Phil. 1:9).

When a person lives in the sphere of love, then he experiences *joy*—that inward peace and sufficiency that is not affected by outward circumstances. (A case in point is Paul's experience recorded in Phil. 4:10-20.) This "holy optimism" keeps him going in spite of difficulties. Love and joy together produce *peace*, "the peace of God, which passeth all understanding" (Phil. 4:7). These first three qualities express the *Godward* aspect of the Christian life.

The next three express the *manward* aspect of the Christian life: *longsuffering* (courageous endurance without quitting), *gentleness* (kindness), and *goodness* (love in action). The Christian who is longsuffering will not avenge himself or wish difficulties on those who oppose him. He will be kind and gentle, even with the most offensive, and will sow goodness where others sow evil. Human nature can never do this on its own; only the Holy Spirit can.

The final three qualities are *selfward: faith* (faithfulness, dependability); *meekness* (the right use of power and authority, power under control); and *temperance* (self-control). Meekness is not weakness. Jesus said, "I am meek and lowly in heart" (Matt. 11:29), and Moses was "very meek" (Num. 12:3); yet no one could accuse either of them of being weak. The meek Christian does not throw his weight around or assert himself. Just as wisdom is the right use of knowledge, so meekness is the right use of authority and power.

It is possible for the old nature to *counterfeit* some of the fruit of the Spirit, but the flesh can never *produce* the fruit of the Spirit. One difference is this: when the Spirit produces fruit, God gets the glory and the Christian is not conscious of his spir-

ituality; but when the flesh is at work, the person
is inwardly proud of himself and is pleased when
others compliment him. The work of the Spirit is
to make us more like Christ for His glory, not for
the praise of men.

The cultivation of the fruit is important. Paul
warns that there must be a right atmosphere before the fruit will grow (vv. 25-26). Just as fruit
cannot grow in every climate, so the fruit of the
Spirit cannot grow in every individual's life or in
every church.

Fruit grows in a climate blessed with an abun-
dance of the Spirit and the Word. "Walk in the
Spirit" (v. 25) means "keep in step with the Spirit"
—not to run ahead and not to lag behind. This involves the Word, prayer, worship, praise, and fellowship with God's people. It also means "pulling
out the weeds" so that the seed of the Word can
take root and bear fruit. The Judaizers were anxious for praise and "vain glory," and this led to
competition and division. Fruit can never grow in
that kind of an atmosphere.

We must remember that this fruit is produced *to
be eaten,* not to be admired and put on display.
People around us are starving for love, joy, peace,
and all the other graces of the Spirit. When they
find them in our lives, they know that we have
something they lack. We do not bear fruit for our
own consumption; we bear fruit that others might
be fed and helped, and that Christ might be glorified. The flesh may manufacture "results" that bring
praise to us, but the flesh cannot bear fruit that
brings glory to God. It takes patience, an atmosphere of the Spirit, walking in the light, the seed
of the Word of God, and a sincere desire to honor
Christ.

In short, the secret is the Holy Spirit. He alone can give us that "fifth freedom"—freedom from sin and self. He enables us to fulfill the law of love, to overcome the flesh, and to bear fruit.

Will you yield to Him and let Him work?

Galatians 6:1-10

Brethren, if a man be overtaken in a fault, ye which are spiritual, restore such an one in the spirit of meekness; considering thyself, lest thou also be tempted.

Bear ye one another's burdens, and so fulfil the law of Christ.

For if a man think himself to be something, when he is nothing, he deceiveth himself. But let every man prove his own work, and then shall he have rejoicing in himself alone, and not in another. For every man shall bear his own burden.

Let him that is taught in the Word communicate unto him that teacheth in all good things.

Be not deceived; God is not mocked: for whatsoever a man soweth, that shall he also reap. For he that soweth to his flesh shall of the flesh reap corruption; but he that soweth to the Spirit shall of the Spirit reap life everlasting.

And let us not be weary in well doing; for in due season we shall reap, if we faint not.

As we have therefore opportunity, let us do good unto all men, especially unto them who are of the household of faith.

11

The Liberty of Love

The story has often been told about the message the founder of the Salvation Army sent to their international convention. General William Booth was unable to attend personally because of ill health, so he cabled the delegates a message containing one word: "OTHERS!"

In the popular comic strip "Peanuts," Lucy asks Charlie Brown, "Why are we here on earth?" He replies, "To make others happy." She ponders this for a moment and then asks, "Then why are the others here?"

"One another" is one of the key phrases in the Christian's vocabulary. "Love one another" is found at least a dozen times in the New Testament, along with "pray one for another" (James 5:16), "edify one another" (1 Thes. 5:11), prefer one another (Rom. 12:10), "use hospitality one to another" (1 Peter 4:9), and many other like admonitions.

In the section before us, Paul adds another phrase: "Bear ye one another's burdens" (Gal. (6:2). The Spirit-led Christian thinks of others and how he can minister to them. In this section, Paul describes two important ministries that we ought to share with one another.

1. Bearing Burdens (6:1-5)

The legalist is not interested in bearing burdens. Instead, he *adds* to the burdens of others (Acts 15:10). This was one of the sins of the Pharisees in Jesus' day: "For they bind heavy burdens and grievous to be borne, and lay them on men's shoulders; but they themselves will not move them with one of their fingers" (Matt. 23:4). The legalist is always harder on other people than he is on himself, but the Spirit-led Christian demands more of himself than he does of others *that he might be able to help others.*

Paul presents a hypothetical case of a believer who is suddenly tripped up and falls into sin. The word *overtaken* carries the idea of being surprised, so it is not a case of deliberate disobedience. Why does Paul use this illustration? *Because nothing reveals the wickedness of legalism better than the way the legalists treat those who have sinned.* Call to mind the Pharisees who dragged a woman taken in adultery before Jesus (John 8). Or that Jewish mob that almost killed Paul because *they thought* he had defiled the temple by bringing in Gentiles (Acts 21:27 ff.). (Legalists do not need facts and proof; they need only suspicions and rumors. Their self-righteous imaginations will do the rest.) So, in this paragraph, Paul is really contrasting the way the legalist would deal with the erring brother, and the way the spiritual man would deal with him.

(1) *A contrast in aim.* The spiritual man would seek to restore the brother in love, while the legalist would exploit the brother. The word *restore* means "to mend, as a net, or to restore a broken

bone." If you have ever had a broken bone, you know how painful it is to have it set. The sinning believer is like a broken bone in the Body, and he needs to be restored. The believer who is led by the Spirit and living in the liberty of grace will seek to help the erring brother, for "the fruit of the Spirit is love" (Gal. 5:22). "By love serve one another" (5:13). When Jesus sought to be a physician to the sinful, He was severely criticized by the Pharisees (Mark 2:13-17), and so the spiritual believer today will be criticized by the legalists.

Instead of trying to restore the erring brother, the legalist will condemn him and then *use the brother to make himself look good.* This is what the Pharisee did in the parable of the Pharisee and the publican (Luke 18:9-14). "[Love] shall cover the multitude of sins" (1 Peter 4:8). The legalist rejoices when a brother falls, and often gives the matter wide publicity, because then he can boast about his own goodness and how much better his group is than the group to which the fallen brother belongs.

This is why Paul admonishes us, "Let us not be desirous of vain glory, provoking one another, envying one another" (Gal. 5:26). The word *provoke* means "to challenge to a contest, to compete with." The believer who walks in the Spirit is not *competing* with other Christians or challenging them to become "as good as he is." However, the legalist lives by competition and comparison, and tries to make himself look good by making the other fellow look bad.

(2) *A contrast in attitude.* The Spirit-led believer approaches the matter in a spirit of meekness and love, while the legalist has an attitude of pride and condemnation. The legalist does not

need to "consider himself" because he pretends he could never commit such a sin. But the believer living by grace realizes that no man is immune from falling. "Let him that thinketh he standeth take heed lest he fall" (1 Cor. 10:12). He has an attitude of humility because he realizes his own weaknesses.

But there is a second contrast: he knows the love of Christ in his own heart. "The law of Christ" is: "Love one another" (John 13:34; 15:12). Paul has already discussed the "law of love" (Gal. 5: 13-15), and now he is applying it. "Tender loving care" is not a modern invention, because Paul is urging it upon believers in this passage. How much we appreciate it when the doctor uses tenderness as he sets a broken bone. And how much more should we use "tender loving care" when we seek to restore a broken life.

It takes a great deal of love and courage for us to approach an erring brother and seek to help him. Jesus compares this to eye surgery (Matt. 7:1-5)—and how many of us feel qualified for that?

Paul probably has in mind here our Lord's instructions on reconciliation (Matt. 18:15-35). If your brother sins against you, go talk to him privately, *not* for the purpose of winning an argument, but for the purpose of winning your brother. (That word *gained* is the same word Paul uses in 1 Cor. 9:19-22 to refer to winning the lost to Christ. It is important to win the lost, but it is also important to win the saved.) If he hears you, then the matter is settled. But if he will not agree, then ask one or two spiritual people to go with you. If he will still not settle the matter, then the whole church must be informed and take steps of discipline. But Jesus goes on to point out that the church must practice prayer (Matt. 18:19-20) and forgiveness (Matt. 18:21-35), or discipline will not be effective.

The legalist, of course, has no time for this kind of spiritual "soul-winning." When he hears that his brother has sinned, instead of going to the brother, he shares the sad news with others ("So you can pray more intelligently about it") and then condemns the brother for not being more spiritual.

Remember, the legalist makes himself look better by making his brother look worse. Thus Paul's warnings here (vv. 3-4). The Judaizers were guilty of boasting about themselves, their achievements, and their converts (Gal. 6:12-14). They usually did this by comparing themselves with others (see (2 Cor. 10:11). But such comparisons are sinful and deceptive. It is easy to find somebody worse off than we are, so that our comparison makes us look better than we really are. Christian love would lead us not to expose a brother's failures or weaknesses, no matter how much better it would make us look.

A man should "prove his own work" (Gal. 6:4) in the light of God's will and not in the shadows of somebody else's achievements. "Each man should test his own actions. Then he can take pride in himself, without comparing himself to somebody else, for each man should carry his own load" (6:4-5, NIV). There is no place for competition in the work of God, unless we are competing against sin and Satan. When we see words like "best, fastest-growing, biggest, finest" applied to Christian ministries, we wonder who is getting the glory.

This does not mean that it is wrong to keep records. Charles Haddon Spurgeon used to say, "Those who criticize statistics usually have none to report." But we must be careful that we are not making others look bad just to make ourselves look good. And we should be able to rejoice at the achievements and blessings of others just as if they were our own (Rom. 12:10). After all, if one member of the Body is blessed, it blesses the whole Body.

There is no contradiction between verses 2 and 5, because two different Greek words for *burden* are used. In verse 2 it is a word meaning "a heavy burden," while in verse 5 it describes "a soldier's pack." We should help each other bear the heavy burdens of life, but there are personal responsibilities that each man must bear for himself. "Each soldier must bear his own pack." If my car breaks down, my neighbor can help drive my children to school, but he cannot assume the responsibilities that only belong to me as their father. That is the difference. It is wrong for me to expect somebody else to be the father in our family; that is a burden (and a privilege) that I alone can bear.

2. Sharing Blessings (6:6-10)

Just as *one another* is a key phrase in the Christian vocabulary, so is the word *fellowship* (translated "communicate" in v. 6). From the very beginning of the church, *sharing* was one of the marks of Christian experience (Acts 2:41-47). The Greek word has now worked its way into our English vocabulary, and we see the word *koinonia* here and there in religious publications. It simply means "to have in common," and refers to our common fellowship in Christ (Gal. 2:9), our common faith (Jude 3), and even our sharing in the sufferings of Christ (Phil. 3:10). But often in the New Testament, *koinonia* refers to the sharing of material blessings with one another (Acts 2:42, 2 Cor.

8:4, Heb. 13:16 [Greek text]). It is this that Paul has in mind in these verses.

He begins with *a precept* (v. 6), urging us to share with one another. The teacher of the Word shares spiritual treasures, and those who are taught ought to share material treasures. (Paul uses a similar approach when he explains why the Gentile churches ought to give an offering to the Jewish believers—Rom. 15:27.) We must remember that what we do with *material* things is an evidence of how we value *spiritual* things. "For where your treasure is, there will your heart be also" (Matt. 6:21).

Because the Apostle Paul did not want money to become a stumbling block to the unsaved, he earned his own living (see 1 Cor. 9), but he repeatedly taught that the spiritual leader in the church was to be supported by the gifts of the people. Jesus said, "The laborer is worthy of his hire" (Luke 10:7), and Paul echoes this statement (1 Cor. 9:11, 14).

But we must realize the spiritual *principle* that lies behind this precept. God does not command believers to give simply that pastors and teachers (and missionaries, Phil. 4:10-19) might have their material needs met, *but that the givers might get a greater blessing* (Gal. 6:7-8). The basic principle of sowing and reaping is found throughout the entire Bible. God has ordained that we *reap what we sow*. Were it not for this law, the whole principle of "cause and effect" would fail. The farmer who sows wheat can expect to reap wheat. If it were otherwise, there would be chaos in our world.

But God has also told us to be careful *where we sow*, and it is this principle that Paul deals with here. He looks upon our material possessions as seed, and he sees two possible kinds of soil: the flesh and the Spirit. We can use our material goods to promote the flesh, or to promote the things of the Spirit. But once we have finished sowing, *we cannot change the harvest.*

Money sown to the flesh will bring a harvest of corruption (see Gal. 5:19-21). That money is gone and can never be reclaimed. Money sown to the Spirit (such as sharing with those who teach the Word) will produce life, and in that harvest will be seeds that can be planted again for another harvest, and on and on into eternity. If every believer only looked upon his material wealth as seed, and planted it properly, there would be no lack in the work of the Lord. Sad to say, much seed is wasted on carnal things and can never bring glory to God.

Of course, there is a much wider application of the principle to our lives; because all that we do is either an investment in the flesh or the Spirit. We shall reap whatever we have sown, and we shall reap *in proportion* as we have sown. "He which soweth sparingly shall reap also sparingly; and he which soweth bountifully shall reap also bountifully" (2 Cor. 9:6). The believer who walks in the Spirit and "sows" in the Spirit is going to reap a spiritual harvest. If his sowing has been generous, the harvest will be bountiful, if not in this life, certainly in the life to come.

Paul's enemies, the Judaizers, did not have this spiritual attitude toward giving and receiving. Paul sacrificed and labored that he might not be a burden to the churches, but the false teachers used the churches to promote their own schemes and fill their own coffers. This is also what happened in the Corinthian church, and Paul had to write them: "In fact, you even put up with anyone who enslaves you or exploits you or takes advantage of you or pushes himself forward or slaps you in the face" (2 Cor. 11:20, NIV).

How many times we have seen the sacrificing godly pastor persecuted and driven out, while the arrogant promoter is honored and gets everything he wants. The carnal believer thrives under the "spiritual dictatorship" of a legalistic promoter-pastor, because it makes him feel secure, successful, and spiritual. The carnal believer will sacrifice what he has to make the work more successful, only to discover that he is sowing to the flesh and not to the Spirit.

Having given us the precept (Gal. 6:6) and the principle behind the precept (vv. 7-8), Paul now gives us *a promise* (v. 9): "In due season we shall reap if we faint not." Behind this promise is a peril: getting weary in the work of the Lord, and then eventually fainting, and stopping our ministry.

Sometimes spiritual fainting is caused by a lack of devotion to the Lord. It is interesting to contrast two churches that are commended for "work, labor, and patience" (1 Thes. 1:3; Rev. 2:2). The church at Ephesus had actually left its first love and was backslidden (Rev. 2:4-5). Why? The answer is seen in the commendation to the Thessalonian church: "Work of faith, labor of love, patience of hope." Not just work, labor, and patience, but the proper motivation: "faith, love, and hope." How easy it is for us to work for the Lord, but permit the spiritual motivation to die. Like the priests of Israel that Malachi addressed, we serve the Lord but complain, "Behold, what a weariness is it" (Mal. 1:13).

Sometimes we faint because of lack of prayer. "Men ought always to pray, and not to faint" (Luke

18:1). Prayer is to the spiritual life what breathing is to the physical life, and if you stop breathing, you will faint. It is also possible to faint because of lack of nourishment. "Man shall not live by bread alone, but by every word that proceedeth out of the mouth of God" (Matt. 4:4). If we try to keep going without proper food and rest, we will faint. How important it is to "wait upon the Lord" to get the strength we need for each day (Isa. 40:28-31).

But the promise Paul gives us will help to keep us going: "In due season we shall reap." The seed that is planted does not bear fruit immediately. There are seasons to the soul just as there are seasons to nature, and we must give the seed time to take root and bear fruit. How wonderful it is when the plowman overtakes the reaper (Amos 9:13). Each day we ought to sow the seed so that one day we will be able to reap (Ps. 126:5-6). But we must remember that the Lord of the harvest is in charge, and not the laborers.

Sharing blessings involves much more than teaching the Word and giving of our material substance. It also involves doing good "unto all men" (Gal. 6:10). There are those in this world who do evil (Ps. 34:16); in fact, there are those who return evil for good (Ps. 35:12). Most of the people in the world return good for good and evil for evil (see 1 Thes. 5:15; Luke 6:32-35). But the Christian is supposed to return good for evil (Rom. 12:18-21) and to do this in a spirit of Christian love. Actually, the Christian's good works are a spiritual sacrifice that he gives to the Lord (Heb. 13:16).

We are to "do good unto all men." This is how we let our light shine and glorify our Father in heaven (Matt. 5:16). It is not only by *words* that we witness to the lost, but also by our *works*. In fact, our works pave the way for our verbal witness; they win us the right to be heard. It is not a question of asking, "Does this person deserve my good works?" Did we deserve what God did for us in Christ? Nor should we be like the defensive lawyer who tried to argue, "Who is my neighbor?" (Luke 10:25-37) Jesus made it very clear that the question is not "Who is my neighbor?" but "To whom can I be a neighbor?"

As we "do good unto all men," we must give priority to "the household of faith," the fellowship of believers. This does not mean that the local church should become an exclusive clique with the members isolated from the world around them and doing nothing to help the lost. Rather, it is a matter of balance. Certainly the believers in Paul's day would have greater needs than would the outsiders, since many of the believers suffered for their faith (see Heb. 10:32-34). Furthermore, a man always cares for his own family before he cares for the neighborhood (1 Tim. 5:8).

We must remember, however, that we share with other Christians so that all of us might be able to share with a needy world. The Christian in the household of faith is a receiver that he might become a transmitter. As we abound in love for one another, we overflow in love for all men (1 Thes. 3:12).

This is how it was meant to be.

Ye see how large a letter I have written unto you with mine own hand.

As many as desire to make a fair show in the flesh, they constrain you to be circumcised; only lest they should suffer persecution for the cross of Christ. For neither they themselves who are circumcised keep the law, but desire to have you circumcised, that they may glory in your flesh.

But God forbid that I should glory, save in the cross of our Lord Jesus Christ, by whom the world is crucified unto me, and I unto the world. For in Christ Jesus neither circumcision availeth anything, nor uncircumcision, but a new creature.

And as many as walk according to this rule, peace be on them, and mercy, and upon the Israel of God.

From henceforth let no man trouble me: for I bear in my body the marks of the Lord Jesus.

Brethren, the grace of our Lord Jesus Christ be with your spirit. Amen.

12

The Marks
of Freedom

It was Paul's custom, after dictating a letter, to take the pen and write his own farewell. His standard signature was, "The grace of our Lord Jesus Christ be with you" (1 Thes. 5:28; see 2 Thes. 3: 17-18). But so concerned is Paul that the Galatians get the message of this letter that he takes the pen and writes *an entire concluding paragraph* with his own hand. "Look at the large letters I write with my own hand!"

Why did Paul write this paragraph, and why did he use such large letters? The Holy Spirit inspired him to add these closing words to give one more contrast between the legalists and the Spirit-led Christians, to show that the Spirit-led believer lives for the glory of God, not the praise of man. And he wrote in large letters for emphasis: "DON'T MISS THIS!"

Some Bible students believe that Paul's thorn in the flesh (2 Cor. 12:7-10; Gal. 4:14-15) was some kind of eye trouble. This would mean that he would have to write in large letters so that he himself would be able to read what he had written.

Whether or not that is true, Paul is making it clear that he has something important to write in conclusion, that he is not simply going to end the letter in some conventional manner. If he did have eye trouble, his willingness to write this closing paragraph with his own hand would certainly appeal to the hearts of the readers.

He has shown them that the believer living under law and the believer living under grace are diametrically opposed to each other. It is not just a matter of "different doctrine," but a matter of two different ways of life. They had to choose between bondage or liberty (Gal. 5:1-12), the flesh or the Spirit (5:13-26), and living for self or living for others (6:1-10).

Now he presents a fourth contrast: living for the praise of men or the glory of God (6:11-18). He is dealing with *motive*, and there is no greater need in our churches today than for an examination of the motives for our ministries. We know *what* we are doing, but do we know *why* we are doing it? A good work is spoiled by a bad motive.

Paul approaches this delicate subject in an interesting way. The legalists wanted to subject the Galatian believers to circumcision, so Paul takes this up and relates it to the work of Christ on the cross, and also to his own ministry. In this paragraph Paul presents three "marked men"—the legalist (6:12-13), the Lord Jesus Christ (6:14-16), and the Apostle Paul himself (6:17-18).

1. The Legalist (6:12-13)

Paul does not have anything good to say about the legalist. He describes him and his kind in four ways.

First, *they are braggarts* (6:12a, 13b). Their main purpose was not to win people to Christ, or even to help the believers grow in grace. Their chief purpose was to win more converts so they could brag about them. They wanted to "make a fine impression outwardly" even though they did no good inwardly. Their work was not done for the good of the church or for the glory of God; it was done for their own glory.

While it is certainly not wrong to want to win people to Christ, or to see the work of the Lord increase, it is definitely wrong to want these blessings for the glory of man. We want to see more people sharing in our ministries, not so that we can count people, but because people count. But we must be careful not to "use people" to further our own selfish programs for our own glorification.

I receive a number of local church newsletters and newspapers. I was shocked to find an article in one of them in which the pastor named several other churches and proceeded to explain how his church was much better. Some of the churches he mentioned were not evangelical in belief, and I wondered what those members would think of Christ and the Gospel if they read his boastful critique. No doubt it made it difficult for the believers to witness to these other people once this pastor had condemned their churches.

Second, *they are compromisers* (6:12b). Why did they preach and practice circumcision and all that went with it? *To escape persecution.* Because Paul preached the grace of God and salvation apart from the works of the law, he was persecuted (Gal. 5:11). The Judaizers tried to make the Christians think that they, too, were Christians, and they tried to make the followers of the Mosaic law think that they, too, obeyed the law. Consequently, they escaped being persecuted by the legalistic group for their identification with the cross of Christ and its devastating effect on the law.

We, today, are prone to look at the cross (and crucifixion) in a sentimental way. We wear crosses on our lapels or on chains around our necks. But to the first-century citizen, the cross was not a beautiful piece of jewelry; it was the lowest form of death and the ultimate humiliation. The proper Roman citizen would never mention the cross in polite conversation. It stood for rejection and shame.

When Paul trusted Christ, he identified himself with the cross and took the consequences. To the Jew the cross was a stumbling block, and to the Gentile it was foolishness (1 Cor. 1:18-31). The legalists, emphasizing circumcision rather than crucifixion, won many converts. Theirs was a popular religion because it avoided the shame of the cross.

Third, *they are persuaders* (6:12a). The word *constrain* carries with it the idea of strong persuasion and even force. It is translated "compel" in Galatians 2:14. While it does not mean "to force against one's will," it is still a strong word. It indicates that the Judaizers were great persuaders; they had a "sales talk" that convinced the Galatian believers that legalism was the way for them. Whenever Paul presented the Word, it was in truth and sincerity, and he used no oratorical tricks or debater's skills. (See 1 Cor. 2:1-5 and 2 Cor. 4:1-5 to see how Paul presented the Word to his listeners. Paul was not a politician; he was an ambassador.)

Fourth, *they are hypocrites* (6:13). "They want you to submit to the law, but they themselves do not obey the law." The legalists belonged to the same group as the Pharisees about whom Jesus said, "They say and do not" (Matt. 23:3). Of course, Paul is not suggesting that the Judaizers *should* keep the law, because keeping the law is neither possible nor necessary. Rather, he is condemning them for their dishonesty; they had no intention of keeping the law, even if they could. Their reverence for the law was only a mask to cover their real goal: winning more converts to their cause. They wanted to report more statistics and get more glory.

Yes, the legalist is a marked man; so when you detect him, avoid him.

2. Jesus Christ (6:14-16)

Paul keeps coming back to the cross (2:20-21; 3:13; 4:5; 5:11, 24; 6:12). "If righteousness come by the law, then Christ is dead in vain" (2:21). The wounds of Calvary certainly make Christ a "marked Man," for those wounds mean liberty to those who will trust Him. The Judaizers boasted in circumcision; but Paul boasted in a crucified and risen Saviour. He gloried in the cross. Certainly this does not mean that he gloried in the brutality or suffering of the cross. He was not looking at the cross as a piece of wood on which a criminal died. He was looking at the cross of *Christ* and glorying in it. Why would Paul glory in the cross?

First, *he knew the Person of the cross.* Jesus Christ is mentioned at least 45 times in the Galatian letter, which means that one-third of the verses contain some reference to Him. The Person of Jesus Christ captivated Paul, and it was Christ who made the cross glorious to him. In his early years as a Jewish rabbi, Paul had much to glory in (Gal. 1: 13-14; Phil. 3:1-10); but after he met Christ, all his self-glory turned to mere refuse. The legalists did not glory in the cross of Christ *because they did not glory in Christ.* It was Moses—and themselves—who got the glory. They did not really know the Person of the cross.

Second, *he knew the power of the cross.* To Saul, the learned Jewish rabbi, a doctrine of sacrifice on a cross was utterly preposterous. That the Messiah would come, he had no doubt, but that He would come to die—and to die *on a cursed cross*—well, there was no place for this in Saul's theology. The cross in that day was the ultimate example of weakness and shame. Yet Saul of Tarsus experienced the power of the cross and became Paul the Apostle. The cross ceased to be a stumbling block to him and became, instead, the very foundation stone of his message: "Christ died for our sins."

For Paul, the cross meant *liberty:* from self (Gal. 2:20), the flesh (5:24), and the world (6:14). In the death and resurrection of Christ the power of God is released to give believers deliverance and victory. It is no longer *we* who live; it is Christ who lives in us and through us. As we yield to Him, we have victory over the world and the flesh. There is certainly no power in the law to give a man victory over self, the flesh, and the law. Quite the contrary, the law *appeals* to the human ego ("I can do something to please God"), and encourages the flesh to work. And the world does not care if we are "religious" just so long as the cross is left out. In fact, the world approves of religion—apart from the Gospel of Jesus Christ. So, the legalist inflates the ego, flatters the flesh, and pleases the world; the true Christian crucifies all three.

Third, *he knew the purpose of the cross.* It was to bring into the world a new "people of God." For centuries, the nation of Israel had been the people of God, and the law had been their way of life. All of this was preparation for the coming of Jesus

Christ (Gal. 4:1-7). Now that Christ had come and finished His great work of redemption, God had set aside the nation of Israel and brought into the world a "new creation" and a new nation, "the Israel of God." This does not mean that God is finished with the nation of Israel. Today, God is calling out from both Jews and Gentiles "a people for His name" (Acts 15:14), and in Christ there are no racial or national distinctions (Gal. 3:27-29). Paul clearly teaches, however, that there is a future in God's plan for the Jewish nation (Rom. 11).

One purpose of the cross was to bring in *a new creation* (Gal. 6:15, NIV). This "new creation" is the Church, the body of Christ. The "old creation" was headed by Adam, and it ended in failure. The new creation is headed by Christ, and it is going to succeed.

To the Romans, Paul explained the doctrine of the two Adams—Adam and Christ (Rom. 5:12-21). The first Adam disobeyed God and brought into the world sin, death, and judgment. The last Adam (1 Cor. 15:45) obeyed God and brought life, righteousness, and salvation. Adam committed one sin and plunged all of creation into judgment. Christ performed one act of obedience in His death on the cross, and paid for all the sins of the world. Because of Adam's sin, death reigns in this world. Because of Christ's victory, *we can "reign in life"* through Jesus Christ (Rom. 5:17). In other words, the believer belongs to a "new creation," a spiritual creation, that knows nothing of the defects and limitations of the "old creation" (see 2 Cor. 5:17).

Another purpose of the cross was to create *a new nation*, "the Israel of God" (Gal. 6:16). This is one of many names for the Church found in the New Testament. Jesus said to the Jewish leaders, "The

kingdom of God shall be taken from you, and given
to a nation bringing forth the fruits thereof" (Matt.
21:43). Peter identifies that nation as the family of
God: "But ye are a chosen generation, a royal
priesthood, an holy nation" (1 Peter 2:9).

As mentioned previously, this does not mean that
the Church has permanently replaced the nation
of Israel in the program of God, but only that the
Church is "the people of God" on earth today just
as Israel was in centuries past.

What a rebuke to the Judaizers. They wanted to
take the Church back into Old Testament law,
when that law could not even be kept by the nation of Israel! That nation was set aside to make
way for God's new people, the Church!

Believers today may not be "Abraham's children"
in the flesh, but they are "Abraham's seed" through
faith in Jesus Christ (Gal. 4:28-29). They have experienced a circumcision of the heart that is far
more effective than physical circumcision (Phil.
3:3; Rom. 2:29; Col. 2:11). For this reason, neither
circumcision nor the lack of it is of any conse-
quence to God (Gal. 6:15; see also 5:6).

3. The Apostle Paul (6:17-18)

There was a time when Paul was proud of his mark
of circumcision (Phil. 3:4-6), but after he became
a believer, he became a "marked man" in a different way. He now gloried in the scars he had received and in the suffering he had endured in the
service of Jesus Christ.

The contrast with the legalists is plain to see:
"The Judaizers want to mark your flesh and brag
about you, but I bear in my body the brands of the
Lord Jesus Christ—for His glory." What a rebuke!
"If your religious celebrities have any scars to show

for the glory of Christ, then let them be shown. Otherwise—stop bothering me!"

Paul is not claiming that he bore the five wounds of Calvary on his body. Rather he is affirming that he has suffered for Christ's sake (something the legalists never did), and he had on his body the scars to prove it. When you read 2 Corinthians 11:18-33, you have no difficulty understanding this claim of his, for in many ways and in many places Paul suffered physically for Christ.

In Paul's day, it was not unusual for the follower of some heathen god or goddess to be branded with the mark of that idol. He was proud of his god and wanted others to know it. In the same way, Paul was "branded" for Jesus Christ. It was not a temporary mark that could be removed, but a permanent mark that he would take to his grave. Nor did he receive his brands in an easy way: he had to suffer repeatedly to become a marked man for Christ.

It was also the practice in that day to brand slaves, so that everyone would know who the owner was. Paul was the slave of Jesus Christ, and he wore His mark to prove it.

It is worth noting that *sin brands a person*. It may mark his mind, his personality, even his body. Few people are proud of the sin marks they bear, and conversion does not change them. (Thank God, those changes will come when Jesus returns!) How much better it is to love Christ and live for Him and be "branded" for His glory.

Believers today need to remember that it is the Christian leader who has *suffered* for Christ who has something to offer. The Judaizers in Paul's day knew nothing of suffering. They may have been persecuted in some small way for belonging to a religious group, but this is far different from "the fellowship of His [Christ's] sufferings" (Phil. 3:10).

Beware of that religious leader who lives in his ivory tower and knows nothing of battling against the world, the flesh, and the devil, who has no "marks" to show for his obedience to Christ. Paul was no armchair general; he was out in the front lines, waging war against sin, and taking his share of suffering.

So, Paul comes to the end of his letter; and he closes just the way he began: GRACE! Not "the law of Moses," but

THE GRACE OF OUR LORD JESUS CHRIST!

No more need be said, because that says it all.

Victor Books
by Warren Wiersbe

Be Complete (Colossians). A study showing how false teachers infiltrated the Colossian church. In this book, the author reminds readers of the preeminence of Christ and of their completeness in Him—6-2726

Be Confident (Hebrews). You can remain unshaken in a shaking society, confident that God is shaking things so you might learn to live by faith—6-2728

Be Encouraged (2 Corinthians). God can turn your trials into triumphs and your sufferings into service—6-2620

Be Faithful (1 & 2 Timothy, Titus). How to be faithful to the Word, your tasks, people who need you—6-2732

Be Free (Galatians). A challenge for you to live in the true freedom you have in Jesus Christ—6-2733

Be Hopeful (1 Peter). We can expect to suffer for our faith, but we can be hopeful. God's grace is ours for the asking!—6-2737

Be Joyful (Philippians). Here are four things that can rob you of joy, and how to overcome them—6-2739

Be Loyal (Matthew). This 26-chapter study examines the life of Christ the King: the miracle of His birth, the compassion of His ministry, and His victory over death—6-2313

Be Mature (James). Learn how you can overcome problems by attaining spiritual maturity—6-2754

Be Ready (1 & 2 Thessalonians). Examine the implications of the doctrine of the Second Coming and the need to get ready for the event—6-2773

Be Real (1 John). Discover the character of true love as revealed in Jesus Christ, with pertinent illustrations that apply truth to life—6-2774

Be Rich (Ephesians). Learn how you can find untold wealth and riches from God—6-2775

Be Right (Romans). A clear and practical exposition of Romans, rich in doctrine and applications for today—6-2778

Be Wise (1 Corinthians). See what a difference it makes when you follow God's wisdom instead of man's knowledge—6-2304

Meet Yourself in the Psalms. From selected psalms, Dr. Wiersbe shows that God gives us new vision and strength to turn tragedy into triumph—6-2740

Windows on the Parables. Look through the parables as a mirror to view our inner selves and an open window to glimpse God—6-2710